JOHN STOTT

A COMPREHENSIVE BIBLIOGRAPHY

Timothy Dudley-Smith

InterVarsity Press
Downers Grove, Illinois

Published in the United States of America by InterVarsity Press, Downers Grove, Illinois, with permission from Universities and Colleges Christian Fellowship, Leicester, England.

InterVarsity Press® is the book-publishing division of InterVarsity Christian Fellowship®, a student movement active on campus at hundreds of universities, colleges and schools of nursing in the United States of America, and a member movement of the International Fellowship of Evangelical Students. For information about local and regional activities, write Public Relations Dept., InterVarsity Christian Fellowship, 6400 Schroeder Rd., P.O. Box 7895, Madison, WI 53707-7895.

ISBN 0-8308-1865-0

Printed in the United States of America ∞

Library of Congress Cataloging-in-Publication Data

Dudley-Smith, Timothy
    John Stott: a comprehensive bibliography covering the years
    1939-1994/compiled by Timothy Dudley-Smith.
       p.   cm.
    Includes index.
    ISBN 0-8308-1865-0 (pbk.: alk. paper)
    1. Stott, John R. W.—Bibliography.   I. Title.
    Z8849.32.S834D83   1996
    [BX5199.S834]
    016.23'03—dc20   95-48954
                                  CIP

16   15   14   13   12   11   10   9   8   7   6   5   4   3   2   1
09   08   07   06   05   04   03   02   01   00   99   98   97   96

Introduction

This is not the first list of John Stott's writings; nor will it be the last. Earlier lists have been prepared by study assistants – notably Toby Howarth in 1987 – and by Frances Whitehead; and a list of books, with brief descriptions, appears as an appendix to the Festschrift published for his 70th birthday, *The Gospel in the Modern World* (edited by Martyn Eden and David F. Wells, IVP, 1991). To all these I am indebted.

But this bibliography is, I think, the first attempt to list John Stott's writings over and above his books and major articles. It is incomplete not only for the reason that, thankfully, he is still writing; but because no comprehensive files or records exist of all that he has so far had published. Material new to me, and unknown or unremembered by him, has come to light at every stage; and further additions must therefore be confidently expected. Equally the list is almost certainly beset by errors, as probably every first bibliography must be; especially when titles are published in more than one country.

I gratefully acknowledge immense help received from almost all the publishers here listed (especially from IVP in the USA, who have published most of the American editions); as well as from a large variety of individuals and from many libraries. I must single out for special mention the libraries and librarians of Oak Hill College, Partnership House, Sion College and Christian Impact, together with the Evangelical Library and the University Library, Cambridge. In America I have had help from the libraries of Princeton Theological Seminary, of both the New Orleans Baptist and the Southwestern Baptist Theological Seminaries and of Wheaton College, as well as from the publishers of *Christianity Today, Decision*, and a host of other journals and symposia. I have had help from Frances Whitehead; from a number of John Stott's study assistants, notably Nelson González; from Carrie Field who originally put the manuscript on to word-processor; from the publishers; and from John Stott himself. Beyond these, I have trespassed on the kindness of individuals too many to list, who I hope will take this general acknowledgment as a sincere expression of thanks.

Because the bibliography is bound to be incomplete I have not numbered items individually, but classified them as books, booklets, contributions to periodicals, and so on, as set out in the table of contents. I think this is self-explanatory apart from two particular points.

First, I distinguish between a book and a booklet by the single physical characteristic of a spine. If the back is a simple fold, no matter how thick, the item is here listed as a booklet or pamphlet. If there is a spine, no matter how thin, it counts for my purpose as a book. Some publications therefore count as a booklet in the UK and a book in the USA, and are listed accordingly as both.

Secondly, and in something of the same way, where John Stott has contributed both a Foreword and a chapter to a symposium, the book will be listed under both headings. If in addition he is the editor, it will appear also in a third.

Because the purpose of the bibliography is to assist those who wish to study John Stott's writings, rather than the book-collector, it contains a minimum of information about different editions; and nothing on dimensions, pagination, or similar matters. However, where earlier books have been republished (not always by the same publisher) in substantially revised and updated editions, these are identified. A few original contributions in languages other than English are listed here; but no attempt is made to include translations. *Basic Christianity* alone would account for over fifty different languages, using a variety of alphabets.

At the back of the bibliography there will be found a list of journals associated with particular churches, colleges or organizations, which may help to identify the provenance of unfamiliar periodicals; and also a united index of contributions by title in alphabetical order, whether of a book, symposium, chapter, review, interview, article or other contribution.

The title page bears the dates 1939–1994, since all the publications listed here fall within that period. If one excludes school magazines, John Stott's writing to date spans fifty years, from 1945 when he was still a student, to the time when this bibliography goes to press. It therefore includes his substantial exposition of *Romans* in 'The Bible Speaks Today' series. Happily, though, John Stott is still writing, and this can therefore only be an interim bibliography, aiming to cover the period shown. Additions and corrections to this first issue will be gratefully received and incorporated, as far as possible, in any future edition.

Timothy Dudley-Smith
Ford, Salisbury
1995

Notes to the User

OMISSIONS

Translations, book-club editions, Bible-reading notes, printed items for private or domestic circulation and letters to the press are generally not included.

ISSUES OF PERIODICALS

All entries are listed in date-order of publication, within their particular classification. For journals, this usually means a cover-date, whether of a quarter, month or particular day. Where the cover gives only a more general indication (Spring, Fall, *etc.*) this is listed in what seems the most appropriate place; and where the only identification is a series number, this again is listed as far as possible in the same chronological order.

CROSS-REFERENCES

Where the same material is published in different forms (whether whole or abridged) a cross-reference forms the link. Usually only the section and date are given, since the number of possible entries to be checked is so few. Occasionally, where it may avoid confusion, a title is added. Cross-references are included from periodicals *etc.* to books; but not usually vice versa.

SERIES OF ARTICLES

Three or more articles or pamphlets linked by subject matter in a reasonably consecutive sequence are listed as a series. Where there is little common thread of subject matter, it would take more than three to constitute a series for this purpose. References to a contribution in a series of articles in a particular journal carry first the reference E(ii), followed by the name of the journal, the dates between which the series ran, and the date of issue of the article in question. Thus 'E(ii):All Souls Sermons 1946–1985; April 1947' will be found to refer to a sermon on Revelation 3:1. Series are listed in date-order *of the first contribution*, regardless of the length of the series as a whole. *All Souls*, the church magazine of All Souls Church, Langham Place, London, has carried at least two lengthy series by John Stott, one of sermons and one of general articles. The name, All Souls, is used throughout to refer both to the church and to the journal, which since September/October 1990 has become the All Souls Broadsheet.

INTERVIEWS

These are included only when John Stott is an actual participant. Descriptions, profiles, assessments, and so on are omitted.

REVIEWS

Occasionally it is difficult to distinguish between a book review and a review article, perhaps as part of a more general series. In such a case, the entry will appear in both sections, with a cross-reference.

TITLES

Titles change with the years. Generally speaking the title of a journal or organization given is that by which it was known at the date in question. Hence the references now to the CSSM and now the Scripture Union; now to the *Church of England Newspaper* and now to the *Church of England Newspaper and Record*; *The Churchman*, for example, became simply *Churchman* in 1977. Titles in alphabets other than Roman are transliterated.

INDEX & RUNNING HEADLINES

The index contains in undifferentiated alphabetical order the titles of books, articles, sermons, and so on. These can be distinguished by the reference given; thus a reference beginning E(ii) would refer to contributions to a series, E(v) to a review, and so on. The index contains titles of works of which John Stott is not the author since it includes the titles of books written or edited by others to which he is a contributor; or of which he is reviewer. Titles of periodicals are not included in the index. The running headline at the top of every recto page contains the key letter of the reference, often followed by a roman numeral (see Table of Contents, p. 5), and covers entries in both verso and recto of that opening. For the order of E(ii) references, please see the note 'Series of Articles' on the facing page.

RECORDINGS

This bibliography does not include the substantial number of recordings available on audio or video cassette of lectures and addresses by John Stott. Something over 300 audio cassette tapes, largely of his sermon ministry at All Souls, are available in the All Souls Tape Library, 2 All Souls Place, London, W1N 3DB, and a further 100 in the tape catalogue of the London Institute of Contemporary Christianity, St Peter's Church, Vere Street, London, W1M 9HP.

The Bibliography

A: Books Written by John Stott

1954

Men with a Message   London: Longmans, 1954.
Grand Rapids: Eerdmans/Downers Grove:
IVP, 1964 under the title *Basic Introduction
to the New Testament*.
The Bishop of London's Lent Book for
1954.
Revised and illustrated edition by Stephen
Motyer, Grand Rapids: Eerdmans, 1994.
See A:1994.

1958

Basic Christianity   London: IVF, 1958; revised 1971.
Grand Rapids: Eerdmans/Downers Grove:
IVP, 1958; revised 1971, see D(iii):1994.

What Christ Thinks   London: Lutterworth, 1958.
of the Church: Grand Rapids: Eerdmans/Downers Grove:
Expository Addresses   IVP, 1959.
on the First Three   Revised and illustrated edition 1990, see
Chapters of the Book   A:1990.
of Revelation
Your Confirmation   London: Hodder & Stoughton, 1958; re-
written 1991.
Part of the 'Christian Commitment' series.
See B(i):1958.
See A:1991, *Christian Basics*.

1959

Fundamentalism and   Grand Rapids: Eerdmans, 1959.
Evangelism   The USA edition in book form of the
pamphlet of the same title, see D(ii):1956.
Reprinted and expanded from two articles
in *Crusade*. See E(iii): November 1955; E(iii):
May 1956.

1961

The Preacher's Portrait: Some New Testament Word Studies	London: Tyndale, 1961. Grand Rapids: Eerdmans/Downers Grove: IVP, 1961. Reissued Downers Grove: IVP, 1991. The 1960 Payton Lectures at Fuller Theological Seminary.

1964

The Baptism and Fullness of the Holy Spirit	Downers Grove: IVP, 1964. The USA edition in book form of the pamphlet of the same title. See D(ii):1964, and (for the revised and enlarged edition) A:1975.
Basic Introduction to the New Testament	See *Men with a Message*, A:1954.
Confess your Sins: The Way of Reconciliation	London: Hodder & Stoughton, 1964. Waco: Word, 1974. The first volume in the 'Christian Foundations' series published under the auspices of the Evangelical Fellowship in the Anglican Communion. See B(i):1964.
The Epistles of John: An Introduction and Commentary	London: Tyndale, 1964. Grand Rapids: Eerdmans/Downers Grove: IVP, 1964. Revised edition based on the NIV text, *The Letters of John*; see A:1988. A volume in the 'Tyndale New Testament Commentaries'. General Editor: Professor R. V. G. Tasker.

1966

The Canticles and Selected Psalms	London: Hodder & Stoughton, 1966. Reprinted in a revised and illustrated edition under the title *Favourite Psalms*. See A:1988. Part of the 'Prayer Book Commentary' series; editor, Frank Colquhoun. See E(ii):Life of Faith 1958.
Men Made New: An Exposition of Romans 5–8	London: IVF, 1966. Downers Grove: IVP, 1966. Reissued Grand Rapids: Baker, 1984.

1967

Our Guilty Silence: London: Hodder & Stoughton, 1967.
The Church, the   Grand Rapids: Eerdmans/Downers Grove:
Gospel and the World   IVP, 1969.
                           The final volume in the 'Christian
                           Foundations' series.
                           See B(i):1964.

1968

The Message of   London: IVP, 1968.
Galatians   Downers Grove: IVP, 1968.
                           The first volume in 'The Bible Speaks
                           Today' series.
                           Reprinted 1973 under the title *Only One
                           Way*; 1984 under the title *The Message of
                           Galatians: Only One Way*; 1989 under the
                           title *Essential Freedom: The Message of
                           Galatians*.
                           See B(i):1968.

1969

One People: Clergy   London: Falcon, 1969.
and Laity in God's   Downers Grove: IVP, 1970.
Church   Revised edition, Old Tappan: Revell, 1982,
                           expanded and updated with the subtitle
                           'Helping your Church Become a Caring
                           Community'.
                           The Pastoral Theology Lectures in Durham
                           University, 1968.

1970

Christ the   London: Tyndale, 1970.
Controversialist: Downers Grove: IVP, 1970.
A Study in some
Essentials of
Evangelical Religion

1971

Christ the Liberator   See C(ii):1971, *Christ the Liberator*.

1972

Understanding the   London: Scripture Union, 1972.
Bible   Ventura: Gospel Light, 1972.

Bombay: Gospel Literature Service, 1973.
Grand Rapids: Zondervan, 1979.
Revised edition, London: Scripture Union,
1976 & 1984.
Grand Rapids: Zondervan, 1984.
Bombay: Gospel Literature Service, 1990.
Sydney: Anzea, n.d.
Reissued in five volumes as 'Key' books,
London: Scripture Union, 1978. See A:1978.
*The Purpose and the Place; The Story of the
Old Testament; The Story of the New Testament;
The Message of Trust; The Bible for Today.*

1973

Guard the Gospel: London: IVP, 1973.
The Message of 2 Downers Grove: IVP, 1973.
Timothy Part of 'The Bible Speaks Today' series.
See B(i):1968.
Reprinted 1984 under the title *The Message
of 2 Timothy: Guard the Gospel.*
See D(iii):1994.

Only One Way Leicester: IVP, 1973.
A reprint of *The Message of Galatians.*
See A:1968.

Your Mind Matters: Downers Grove: IVP, 1973.
The Place of the Mind The USA edition in book form of the
in the Christian Life pamphlet of the same title. See D(ii):1972.

1975

Baptism and Fullness: London: IVP, 1975.
The Work of the Holy Downers Grove: IVP, 1976.
Spirit Today The revised and enlarged version of the
booklet *The Baptism and Fullness of the Holy
Spirit.* See D(ii):1964.

Christian Mission in London: Falcon, 1975.
the Modern World Reissued Eastbourne: Kingsway, 1986.
Downers Grove: IVP, 1975, with the
subtitle 'What the Church should be Doing
Now!'
Bombay: Gospel Literature Service, n.d.
The 1974 Chavasse Lectures at Wycliffe
Hall, Oxford.

The Lausanne Covenant: An Exposition and Commentary	Charlotte: Worldwide Publications, 1975. The USA edition in book form of the pamphlet of the same title. See D(ii):1975.

1978

Christian Counter-Culture: The Message of the Sermon on the Mount	Leicester: IVP, 1978. Downers Grove: IVP, 1978. Part of 'The Bible Speaks Today' series, expounding Matthew 5–7. Reprinted 1985 under the title *The Message of the Sermon on the Mount*. See B(i):1968.
The Purpose and the Place	London: Scripture Union, 1978.
The Story of the Old Testament	London: Scripture Union, 1978.
The Story of the New Testament	London: Scripture Union, 1978.
The Message to Trust	London: Scripture Union, 1978.
The Bible for Today	London: Scripture Union, 1978. See A:1972. A series entitled 'Key Books', being reprints of individual chapters from *Understanding the Bible*.

1979

Focus on Christ: An Enquiry into the Theology of Prepositions	London: Collins, 1979. Cleveland, Ohio: Collins, 1979. Reissued Grand Rapids: Zondervan, 1981 under the title *Understanding Christ*. Revised and illustrated edition under the title *Life in Christ*. See A:1991.
God's New Society: The Message of Ephesians	Leicester: IVP, 1979. Downers Grove: IVP, 1980. Part of 'The Bible Speaks Today' series. Reprinted 1984 under the title *The Message of Ephesians: God's New Society*; 1989 under the title *Essential Fellowship: The Message of Ephesians*. See B(i):1968.
Understanding Christ	See above: *Focus on Christ*.

1982

Between Two Worlds: The Art of Preaching in the Twentieth Century	See below: *I Believe in Preaching*.
The Bible: Book for Today	Leicester: IVP, 1982. Downers Grove: IVP, 1983 under the title *God's Book for God's People*. Reissued Grand Rapids: Discovery House, 1991 under the title *You Can Trust the Bible*. See A:1991.
I Believe in Preaching	London: Hodder & Stoughton, 1982. Grand Rapids: Eerdmans, 1982 under the title *Between Two Worlds*. Bombay: Gospel Literature Service, 1988. Part of the 'I Believe' series; editor: Michael Green.

1983

God's Book for God's People	Downers Grove: IVP, 1983. See A:1982, *The Bible: Book for Today*.

1984

Issues Facing Christians Today	London: Marshalls, 1984. Old Tappan: Revell, 1985 under the title *Involvement*, in 2 volumes. Bombay: Gospel Literature Service, 1988. Revised and enlarged edition, London: Collins/Marshall Pickering, 1990. Old Tappan: Revell, 1990 under the title *Decisive Issues Facing Christians Today*.
The Message of Ephesians: God's New Society	Leicester: IVP, 1984. See A:1979, *God's New Society: The Message of Ephesians*.
The Message of Galatians: Only One Way	Leicester: IVP, 1984. See A:1968, *The Message of Galatians*.
The Message of 2 Timothy: Guard the Gospel	Leicester: IVP, 1984. See A:1973, *Guard the Gospel: The Message of 2 Timothy*. See D(iii):1994.

1985

The Authentic Jesus: A Response to Current Scepticism in the Church	London: Marshalls, in conjunction with the London Institute for Contemporary Christianity, 1985. Downers Grove: IVP, 1985. Part of the 'Contemporary Christian Issues' series. See B(i):1985.
Involvement, Vol. 1: Being a Responsible Christian in a Non-Christian Society	Old Tappan: Revell, 1985. See A:1984, *Issues Facing Christians Today.*
Involvement, Vol. 2: Social and Sexual Relationships in the Modern World	Old Tappan: Revell, 1985. See A:1984, *Issues Facing Christians Today.*

1986

The Cross of Christ	Leicester: IVP, 1986. Downers Grove: IVP, 1986.
The Whole Christian (in Korean)	Seoul: Korea Inter-Varsity Press, 1986. Reprinted from the *Proceedings of the International Conference of Christian Medical Students, 1980.* See C(ii):1980.

1988

Essentials: A Liberal-Evangelical Dialogue	London: Hodder & Stoughton, 1988. Downers Grove: IVP, 1989 under the title *Evangelical Essentials.* By David L. Edwards and John Stott.
Favourite Psalms	Milton Keynes: Word, 1988. Chicago: Moody, 1988. Willowdale, Ontario: R. G. Mitchell Family Books, 1988. See D(iii):1994. A revised and illustrated edition of *The Canticles and Selected Psalms.* See A:1966.
The Letters of John	See A:1964, *The Epistles of John.*

1989

Essential Fellowship: The Message of Ephesians	Leicester: IVP, 1989. A reprint of *God's New Society: The Message of Ephesians.* See A:1979.

Essential Freedom:	Leicester: IVP, 1989.
The Message of	A reprint of *The Message of Galatians.*
Galatians	See A:1968.
Evangelical	Downers Grove: IVP, 1989.
Essentials:	See A:1988, *Essentials.*
A Liberal-Evangelical	
Dialogue	

1990

Decisive Issues	See A:1984, *Issues Facing Christians Today.*
Facing Christians	
Today	
The Lordship of	Pietermaritzburg: Africa Enterprise, 1990.
Christ in South	The substance of six lectures given in some
Africa	major cities of South Africa during 1988;
	later to form part of the text of *The*
	Contemporary Christian. See A:1992.
The Message of Acts:	Leicester: IVP, 1990.
To the Ends of the	Downers Grove: IVP, 1990 under the title
Earth	*The Spirit, the Church and the World.*
	Part of 'The Bible Speaks Today' series.
	See B(i):1968.
The Spirit, the	See immediately above: *The Message of Acts:*
Church and the	*To the Ends of the Earth.*
World	
What Christ Thinks	Milton Keynes: Word, 1990.
of the Church	Wheaton: Harold Shaw, 1990.
	A revised and illustrated edition of the
	earlier book of the same title. See A:1958.

1991

Christian Basics:	Grand Rapids: Baker, 1991.
A Handbook of	The 1991 edition of *Your Confirmation*
Beginnings, Beliefs	(see A:1958), adapted for an
and Behaviour	interdenominational USA readership.
The Gospel and the	Downers Grove: IVP, 1991.
End of Time	See below: *The Message of Thessalonians:*
	Preparing for the Coming King.
Life in Christ	Eastbourne: Kingsway, 1991.
	Wheaton: Tyndale House, 1991.
	A revised and illustrated edition of *Focus*
	on Christ. See A:1979.

The Message of Thessalonians: Preparing for the Coming King	Leicester: IVP, 1991. Downers Grove: IVP, 1991 under the title *The Gospel and the End of Time*. Part of 'The Bible Speaks Today' series. See B(i):1968.
You Can Trust the Bible: Our Foundation for Belief and Obedience	Grand Rapids: Discovery House, 1991. See A:1982, *The Bible: Book for Today*.

1992

The Contemporary Christian: An Urgent Plea for Double Listening	Leicester: IVP, 1992. Downers Grove: IVP, 1992 with the subtitle 'Applying God's Word to Today's World'. A companion volume to *Issues Facing Christians Today*. See A:1984; D(iii):1994.
Los Problemas del Liderazgo Cristiano (Problems of Christian Leadership)	Buenos Aires: Ediciones Certeza Abua, 1992.

1994

Men with a Message: An Introduction to the New Testament and its Writers	Grand Rapids: Eerdmans, 1994. Revised by Stephen Motyer. See A:1954.
The Message of Romans: God's Good News for the World	Leicester: IVP, 1994. Downers Grove: IVP, 1994 under the title *Romans: God's Good News for the World*. Part of 'The Bible Speaks Today' series. See B(i):1968.

B: Books edited by John Stott

(i) Series

Including series wholly written by John Stott.

1958

The 'Christian Commitment' series	London: Hodder & Stoughton, 1958. Five titles, including *Your Confirmation* by John Stott, prepared under his general

direction. See A:1958, *Your Confirmation*.
See B(ii):1994 and C(i):1994 for new edition
of *Your Marriage*.

1964

The 'Christian
Foundations' series

London: Hodder & Stoughton, 1964–1967.
Twenty-two titles, including *Confess Your
Sins*, 1964 and *Our Guilty Silence*, 1967 by
John Stott.
Editors: Philip E. Hughes and Frank
Colquhoun.
Produced under the auspices of the
Literature Committee of the Evangelical
Fellowship in the Anglican Communion
chaired by John Stott.
See A:1964; A:1967.

1968

'The Bible Speaks
Today' series

London: IVP, 1968–   .
Downers Grove: IVP, 1968–
Editors: J. A. Motyer (Old Testament) and
John Stott (New Testament).
See A:1968, *The Message of Galatians*; A:1973,
Guard the Gospel: The Message of 2 Timothy;
A:1978, *Christian Counter-Culture: The
Message of the Sermon on the Mount*; A:1979,
God's New Society: The Message of Ephesians;
A:1990, *The Message of Acts: To the Ends of the
Earth*; A:1991, *The Message of Thessalonians:
Preparing for the Coming King*; A:1994, *The
Message of Romans: God's Good News for the
World*. (In preparation: *1 Timothy and Titus*.)

1977

'Obeying Christ in a
Changing World'
series

London: Collins, 1977.
Three titles, each containing John Stott's
General Introduction. Volume 1, *The Lord
Christ*, was edited by John Stott and
includes his chapter with the same title as
the series, of which he was General Editor.
Published as part of the preparation for the
second National Evangelical Anglican
Congress, Nottingham 1977.
See B(ii):1977; C(i):1977; C(ii):1977.

1978

'Key Books' series   London: Scripture Union, 1978.
                      Ventura: Gospel Light, 1978.
                      Five titles, all by John Stott, reprinted from
                      his book *Understanding the Bible*. See
                      A:1972; A:1978.

1985

The 'Contemporary   London: Marshalls and the London Institute
Christian Issues'   for Contemporary Christianity, 1985.
series   Three titles, two booklets and a book all by
                     John Stott; two (*Abortion* and *A Call to
                     Christian Leadership*) taken from his book
                     Issues Facing Christians Today; and a third
                     The Authentic Jesus, subtitled 'A Response to
                     Current Scepticism in the Church'. See A:1985;
                     D(i):1985; D(ii):1985.

(ii) Individual Titles

1977

Das Himmelreich hat   Wuppertal: Rolf Brockhaus, 1977.
Schon Begonnen: Editors: John Stott and Klaas Runia.
Reich Gottes in   Papers given at the Conference of the
Unserer Zeit   Fellowship of European Evangelical
(The Kingdom of   Theologians, September 1976.
Heaven has already   See C(i):1977; C(ii):1977.
Begun: The
Kingdom of God in
our Time)
The Lord Christ   London: Collins, 1977.
                         See B(i):1977, 'Obeying Christ in a
                         Changing World'.
                         See C(i):1977; C(ii):1977.

1980

Crime and the   London: Hodder & Stoughton, 1980.
Responsible   Grand Rapids: Eerdmans, 1981.
Community   Editors: John Stott and Nick Miller.
                         The London Lectures in Contemporary
                         Christianity, 1979, by Charles Colson,
                         Norman Anderson, David McNee and
                         others. See C(i):1980.

Down to Earth:	Grand Rapids: Eerdmans, 1980.
Studies in	London: Hodder & Stoughton, 1981.
Christianity and	Editors: John Stott and Robert T. Coote.
Culture	An abridgement of *Gospel and Culture*, 1979; the papers of the Lausanne Consultation at Willowbank, Bermuda, January 1978. See C(i):1979, 1980.

1983

The Year 2000 A.D.	London: Marshalls, 1983. Downers Grove: IVP, 1983. Title in USA: *The Year 2000*. The London Lectures in Contemporary Christianity 1981; with a Foreword by the Editor. See C(i):1983.

1984

Free to be Different	London: Marshalls, 1984. The London Lectures in Contemporary Christianity, 1982 by Malcolm Jeeves, R. J. Berry and David Atkinson, with a Foreword by the Editor. See C(i):1984.

1986

The Evangelical –	Exeter: Paternoster, 1986.
Roman Catholic	Grand Rapids: Eerdmans, 1986.
Dialogue on Mission,	Editors: John Stott and Basil Meeking.
1977–1984: A Report	See E(iii): January 1986.

1987

Stepping Stones:	London: Hodder & Stoughton, 1987.
Joint Essays on	Editor: Christina Baxter.
Anglican Catholic	Consulting Editors: John Stott and Roger
and Evangelical	Greenacre.
Unity	See C(i):1987; C(ii):1987.

1994

Your Marriage	London: Hodder & Stoughton, 1994. By Michael and Myrtle Baughen. See B(i): 1958, the 'Christian Commitment' series; C(i):1994. Re-written by new authors, this replaces the title *Your Marriage* from the 1958 series.

C: Contributions to Books

(i) Forewords, Introductions, etc.

1954

John Sung   London: China Inland Mission, 1954.
                               By Leslie T. Lyall.
                               Foreword by John Stott.

1964

Pioneers of the   London: Church Book Room Press, 1964.
Reformation in   By Marcus L. Loane.
England   Foreword by John Stott.

1967

You in Your Small   London: IVF, 1967.
Corner   By Ralph Capenerhurst.
                               Foreword by John Stott.

1968 and onwards

'The Bible Speaks   London & Leicester: IVP, 1968–
Today' series   Downers Grove: IVP, 1968– .
                             From the second title in this series (*Guard
                             the Gospel: The Message of 2 Timothy*, 1973)
                             each volume in this series has contained a
                             General Introduction, in the same words,
                             by John Stott as Series Editor; latterly
                             signed by J. A. Motyer as Series Editor
                             (OT) and John R. W. Stott as Series Editor
                             (NT). See B(i):1968.

1972

Ethiopian Jews   London: The Olive Press, 1972.
                             By Eric Payne.
                             Foreword by John Stott.

1976

The New Face of   London: Hodder & Stoughton, 1976.
Evangelicalism   Downers Grove: IVP, 1976.
                             Editor: C. René Padilla.
                             An international symposium on the
                             Lausanne Covenant.
                             Foreword by John Stott. See C(ii): 1976.

1977

Christ and the Media	London: Hodder & Stoughton, 1977.
	By Malcolm Muggeridge.
	The London Lectures in Contemporary
	Christianity, 1976.
	Preface by John Stott.
	Chairman's speech by John Stott.

Das Himmelreich hat Wuppertal: Rolf Brockhaus, 1977.
Schon Begonnen: Editors: John Stott and Klaas Runia.
Reich Gottes in Papers given at the Conference of the
Unserer Zeit Fellowship of European Evangelical
(The Kingdom of Theologians, September 1976.
Heaven has already Vorwort by John Stott (Foreword by John
Begun: The Stott).
Kingdom of God in See B(ii): 1977; C(ii):1977.
our Time)

The Nottingham London: Falcon, 1977.
Statement The official statement of the second
National Evangelical Congress,
Nottingham, April 1977.
Preface by John Stott.

'Obeying Christ in a London: Collins, 1977.
Changing World' Each of the three titles in this series
series contains the same General Introduction by
John Stott as General Editor.
The titles are:
The Lord Christ, editor: John Stott
The People of God, editor: Ian Cundy
The Changing World, editor: Bruce Kaye.
See B(i):1977; C(ii):1977.

1979

Gospel and Culture Pasadena: William Carey Library, 1979.
The papers of the 'Willowbank Consultation'
on Gospel and Culture, January 1978 under
the auspices of the Lausanne Committee
for World Evangelization.
Preface by John Stott.

Human Science and London: Hodder & Stoughton, 1979.
Human Dignity By Donald MacKay.
The London Lectures in Contemporary
Christianity, 1977.
Foreword by John Stott.

1980

Crime and the	London: Hodder & Stoughton, 1980.
Responsible	Grand Rapids: Eerdmans, 1981.
Community	By Charles Colson, Norman Anderson, David McNee and others.
	The London Lectures in Contemporary Christianity, 1979.
	Foreword by John Stott. See B(ii):1980.
Down to Earth:	Grand Rapids: Eerdmans, 1980.
Studies in	London: Hodder & Stoughton, 1981.
Christianity and	Editors: John Stott and Robert T. Coote.
Culture	An abridgement of *Gospel and Culture*.
	See B(ii):1980; C(i):1979.
	Foreword by John Stott.

1982

Evangelism and	Exeter: Paternoster, 1982 on behalf of the
Social Responsibility:	Lausanne Committee for World
An Evangelical	Evangelization and the World Evangelical
Commitment	Fellowship.
	The Report on the International Consultation on the Relationship between Evangelism and Social Responsibility, Grand Rapids, Michigan, June 1982.
	Foreword by John Stott.
	Also issued as Lausanne Occasional Paper No. 21.
The Gift of Helping	Leicester: IVP, 1982.
	By Myra Chave-Jones.
	Foreword by John Stott.
Lifestyle in the	Philadelphia: Westminster Press, 1982.
Eighties	Editor: Ronald J. Sider.
	Papers presented at the International Consultation on Simple Lifestyle, held at Hoddesden, England, 17–21 March, 1980.
	Preface by John Stott and Ronald J. Sider.
Morality and the	London: Hodder & Stoughton, 1982.
Market Place	By Brian Griffiths.
	The London Lectures in Contemporary Christianity, 1980.
	Foreword by John Stott.

1983

Masters of the English Reformation	London: Hodder & Stoughton, 1983. By Marcus L. Loane. First published 1954 by Church Book Room Press. Foreword (in this edition only) by John Stott.
The Year 2000 A.D.	London: Marshalls, 1983. Downers Grove: IVP, 1983. Title in USA: *The Year 2000.* The London Lectures in Contemporary Christianity, 1981, seven contributors. Foreword by John Stott. See B(ii):1983.

1984

Free to be Different	London: Marshalls, 1984. By Malcolm Jeeves, R. J. Berry and David Atkinson. The London Lectures in Contemporary Christianity, 1982. Foreword by John Stott. See B(ii):1984.
God's Word in a Young World	London: Scripture Union, 1984. By Nigel Sylvester. Foreword by John Stott.

1986

Decide for Peace: Evangelicals Against the Bomb	London: Marshall Pickering, 1986. Editor: Dana Mills-Powell. Foreword by John Stott.
Evangelical Preaching	Portland: Multnomah Press, 1986. Sermons by Charles Simeon. Introduction, 'Charles Simeon: a personal appreciation', by John Stott.
Introducing Jesus	Eastbourne: Kingsway, 1986. By Roy Clements. Foreword by John Stott.

1987

Stepping Stones: Joint Essays on Anglican Catholic and Evangelical Unity	London: Hodder & Stoughton, 1987. Editor: Christina Baxter. Consulting Editors: John Stott and Roger Greenacre. Preface by Roger Greenacre and John Stott. See B(ii):1987; C(ii):1987.

1991

For Christ and the University	Downers Grove: IVP, 1991. By Keith and Gladys Hunt. Foreword by John Stott. See C(ii):1991.

1993

Awakening to a World of Need	Leicester: IVP, 1993. By Timothy Chester. Foreword by John Stott.
New Age versus the Gospel	Grantham, Lincs: Autumn House, 1993. By David Marshall. Introduction, 'Conflicting Gospels', by John Stott abridged from the *Church of England Newspaper*. See E(iii): 8 December 1989.
Under the Bright Wings	London: Hodder & Stoughton, 1993. By Peter Harris. Foreword by John Stott.

1994

Your Marriage	London: Hodder & Stoughton, 1994. By Michael and Myrtle Baughen. Foreword by John Stott. See B(i):1958, the 'Christian Commitment' series; B(ii):1994.

(ii) Chapters, Articles, etc.

1955

The Church Extends her Frontiers	London: Marshall, Morgan & Scott, 1955. The Report of the 121st Islington Clerical Conference, January 1955. 'The Church's Continuing Mission in the Parish'.

1957

Annual Report of the Church Pastoral-Aid Society	London: CPAS, 1957. The Annual Sermon preached by John Stott in All Souls, 2 October 1956 from 2 Corinthians 4:1–2, 'We Faint Not'.

1962

The Keswick Week, 1962	London: Marshall, Morgan & Scott, 1962. Editor: H. F. Stevenson. Addresses from the 1962 Keswick Convention. 'The Calling of the Church: Studies in 1 Corinthians 1–6'. i. 'Its Unity' ii. 'Its Humility' iii. 'Its Ministry' iv. 'Its Purity' Sermon: 'Two Great Privileges of Being a Christian'.

1963

The Best of Crusade	London: Victory Press, 1963. Editor: David Winter. 'The Power of God'. From a sermon in All Souls. See E(ii):All Souls Sermons 1964–1985; April 1962.

1964

The Anglican Synthesis: Essays by Catholics and Evangelicals	Derby: Peter Smith, 1964. Editor: W. R. F. Browning. 'The Evangelical Doctrine of Baptism'.

1965

The Keswick Week, 1965	London: Marshall, Morgan & Scott, 1965. Editor: H. F. Stevenson. Addresses from the 1965 Keswick Convention. 'The Privileges of the Justified: Studies in Romans 5–8'. i. 'Peace with God' ii. 'Union with Christ' iii. 'Freedom from the Law' iv. 'Life in the Spirit' See A:1966, *Men Made New*. Sermon: 'The Holy Spirit and Christian Holiness'.

Change, Witness, Triumph	Downers Grove: IVP, 1965. Editors: Paul Fromer and Ellen Weldon. Addresses from the Inter-Varsity missionary convention, Urbana, 1964. 'Christian Ministry: Studies in 2 Corinthians 1–6'. i. 'Christian Ministry: our Privilege' ii. 'Christian Ministry: our Problems' iii. 'Christian Ministry: our Motives and Message' iv. 'Christian Ministry: our Responsibilities'

1966

Bishops in the Church	London: Church Book Room Press, 1966. Editor: R. P. Johnston. Addresses from the 132nd Islington Clerical Conference, January 1966. 'The New Testament Concept of Episkope: An Exposition of Acts 20:17–38'.

1967

Guidelines	London: Falcon, 1967. Editor: J. I. Packer. Essays in preparation for the first National Evangelical Anglican Congress, Keele, 1967. 'Jesus Christ our Teacher and Lord'.
Hard Questions	London: Falcon, 1967. Editor: Frank Colquhoun. 'Was it Necessary for Jesus to Die on the Cross?'
One Race, One Gospel, One Task: World Congress on Evangelism, Berlin, 1966, Vol. 1	Minneapolis: World Wide Publications, 1967. Editors: Carl F. H. Henry and W. Stanley Mooneyham. 'The Great Commission'. See E(ii): Christianity Today 1968.

1968

God's Men: From All Nations to All Nations	Downers Grove: IVP, 1968. Addresses from the Inter-Varsity missionary convention, Urbana, 1967. 'God's Man: Studies in 2 Timothy'. i. 'The Charge to Guard the Gospel'

ii. 'The Charge to Suffer for the Gospel'
iii. 'The Charge to Continue in the Gospel'
iv. 'The Charge to Preach the Gospel'
See A:1973, *Guard the Gospel: The Message of 2 Timothy*.

1969

The Keswick Week, 1969	London: Marshall, Morgan & Scott, 1969. Editor: H. F. Stevenson. Addresses from the 1969 Keswick Convention. 'God's Man: Studies in 2 Timothy'. i. 'The Charge to Timothy to Guard the Gospel' ii. 'The Charge to Timothy to Suffer for the Gospel' iii. 'The Charge to Timothy to Continue in the Gospel' iv. 'The Charge to Timothy to Preach the Gospel' See A:1973, *Guard the Gospel: The Message of 2 Timothy*.

1971

Christ the Liberator	Downers Grove: IVP, 1971. London: Hodder & Stoughton, 1972. Addresses from the Inter-Varsity missionary convention, Urbana, 1970. Authorship listed as 'John Stott and others'. 'The Upper Room Discourse: John's Gospel, 13–17'. i. 'The Foot-washing Lord and Saviour' ii. 'The Two Comings of Christ' iii. 'The Threefold Duty of the Christian' iv. 'The Master's Final Prayer' See D(iii):1994.
Prophecy in the Making	Carol Stream: Creation House, 1971. Editor: Carl F. H. Henry. Messages prepared for the Jerusalem Conference on Biblical Prophecy, June 1971. 'The Gospel and the Nations.'

1972

The Eye of the Storm: The Great Debate in Mission	Chicago: World Books, 1972. Editor: Donald McGavran. 'Does Section Two Provide Sufficient Emphasis on World Evangelism?'
The Keswick Week, 1972	London: Marshall, Morgan & Scott, 1972. Editor: H. F. Stevenson. Addresses from the 1972 Keswick Convention. 'Christ's Portrait of a Christian: Studies in Matthew 5, 6 & 7'. i. 'A Christian's Character' ii. 'A Christian's Righteousness' iii. 'A Christian's Ambition' iv. 'A Christian's Relationships' See A:1978, *Christian Counter-Culture: The Message of the Sermon on the Mount.* Sermon: 'The Spirit in the Believer'.
Die Kommende Ökumene: Theologische Untersuchungen (The Coming World Church: Theological Explorations)	Wuppertal: Rolf Brockhaus, 1972. Editor: H. Richter. A Festschrift for Professor Dr. J. W. Winterhager. 'Evangelicals in the Church of England: a Historical and Contemporary Survey'.

1973

Evangelicals Today	London: Lutterworth, 1973. Editor: John C. King. 'World-wide Evangelical Anglicanism'.

1974

Jesus Christ: Lord of the Universe, Hope of the World	Downers Grove: IVP, 1974. Editor: David M. Howard. Addresses from the Inter-Varsity missionary convention, Urbana, 1973. 'Jesus Christ and the Authority of the Word of God'. Sermon: 'The Key to Missionary Advance'. See D(ii):1974.

Vocation and Victory: An International Symposium presented in honour of Erik Wickberg, General of the Salvation Army.	Basle, Switzerland: Brunnen Publishing House, 1974. Editors: J. W. Winterhager and Arnold Brown. 'The Rise and Fall of Missionary Concern in the Ecumenical Movement, 1910–1973'.

1975

The Keswick Week, 1975	London: Marshall, Morgan & Scott, 1975. Editor: H. F. Stevenson. Addresses from the 1975 Keswick Convention. 'God's New Society: Studies in Ephesians'. i. 'New Life' ii. 'New Society' iii. 'New Standards' iv. 'New Relationships' See A:1984, *The Message of Ephesians: God's New Society*.
Let the Earth Hear His Voice	Minneapolis: World Wide Publications, 1975. Editor: J. D. Douglas. Papers and responses of the Lausanne International Congress on World Evangelization, 1974. 'Introduction to Covenant'. 'The Biblical Basis of Evangelism'.
Mission Trends No. 2: Evangelization	New York: Paulist Press / Grand Rapids: Eerdmans, 1975. Editors: Gerald H. Anderson and Thomas F. Stransky. 'The Biblical Basis of Evangelism'. Reprinted from *Let the Earth hear His Voice*. See immediately above, C(ii):1975.

1976

Jesus Christus Befreit und Eint: Fünfte Vollversammlung des Ökumenischen Rates der Kirchen in Nairobi (Jesus Christ Frees and Unites: Fifth Assembly of the World Council of Churches in Nairobi)

Frankfurt: Lembeck Verlag, 1976.
Editor: Hanfried Kruger.
'Reply to Mortimer Arias: "Damit die Welt Glaube" ' (Reply to Mortimer Arias: 'That the World may Believe').

The New Face of Evangelicalism

London: Hodder & Stoughton, 1976.
Downers Grove: IVP, 1976.
Editor: C. René Padilla.
An international symposium on the Lausanne Covenant.
'The Authority and Power of the Bible'.
See C(i):1976.

Ökumene im Spiegel von Nairobi, '75 (Ecumenism in the Light of Nairobi, '75)

Bad Liebenzell: Liebenzeller Mission, 1976.
Editors: Peter Beyerhaus and Ulrich Betz.
'Antwort auf die Ansprache von Bischof Mortimer Arias' (A Reply to the Address of Bishop Mortimer Arias).

1977

Das Himmelreich hat Schon Begonnen: Reich Gottes in Unserer Zeit (The Kingdom of Heaven has already Begun: The Kingdom of God in our Time)

Wuppertal: Rolf Brockhaus, 1977.
Editors: John Stott and Klaas Runia.
Papers given at the Conference of the Fellowship of European Evangelical Theologians, September 1976.
'Reich Gottes und Gemeinschaft' (The Kingdom of God and Society).
See B(ii):1977 and C(i):1977.

Death: Jesus made it all Different

New Canaan: Keats Publishing, Inc., 1977.
Editor: Miriam G. Moran.
'Beyond the Divide'.
From a sermon in All Souls.
See E(ii):All Souls Sermons 1946–1985; February 1964.

Declare His Glory among the Nations	Downers Grove: IVP, 1977. Editor: David M. Howard. Addresses from the Inter-Varsity missionary convention, Urbana, 1976. 'The Biblical Basis for Declaring God's Glory'. i. 'The Living God is a Missionary God' ii. 'The Lord Christ is a Missionary Christ' iii. 'The Holy Spirit is a Missionary Spirit' iv. 'The Christian Church is a Missionary Church'
The Lord Christ	London: Collins, 1977. Editor and General Editor: John Stott. The first volume in the series 'Obeying Christ in a Changing World'. See B(i):1977; B(ii):1977.
Our Sovereign God	Grand Rapids: Baker, 1977. Editor: James M. Boice. Addresses presented to the Philadelphia Conference on Reformed Theology, 1974–1976. 'The Sovereignty of God the Son'. 'The Sovereign God and the Church'.

1978

The Christian at Work Overseas	Teddington: Tear Fund, 1978. Editor: Ian Prior. 'Mission'. Abridged from chapter 1 of *Christian Mission in the Modern World*. See A:1975.
Essays in Evangelical Social Ethics	Exeter: Paternoster, 1978. Editor: David F. Wright. Epilogue: 'Tasks which Await Us'.
Evangelical Roots	Nashville: Thomas Nelson, 1978. Editor: Kenneth S. Kantzer. A tribute to Wilbur Smith. 'Biblical Preaching is Expository Preaching'.
Facing the New Challenges	Kisumu, Kenya: Evangel Publishing House, 1978. The message of the Pan–African Christian Leadership Assembly. 'Theological Tension Points in Ecumenical–Evangelical Relationships'.

'The Living God is a Missionary God'.
'The Lord Christ is a Missionary Christ'.
See C(ii):1977, *Declare His Glory among the Nations*.

The Gospel, the Spirit, the Church
Bromley: STL Books, 1978.
Editor: David Porter.
Addresses from the Keswick Convention, 1978.
'Gospel and Church: Lessons from First Thessalonians'.
i. 'Christian Evangelism: How the Gospel Spreads'
ii. 'Christian Ministry: How Pastors Serve both Word and People'
iii. 'Christian Standards: How to Please God More and More'
iv. 'Christian Community: How to Care for Each Other in the Church Family'
See A:1991, *The Message of Thessalonians: Preparing for the Coming King*.
Sermon: 'The Lordship of Christ'.

Someone Who Beckons
Leicester: IVP, 1978.
Downers Grove: IVP, 1978.
London: Hodder & Stoughton, 1994.
By Timothy Dudley-Smith.
Extract from *Walk in His Shoes*. See D(ii):1975.

1979

You Can Tell the World
Downers Grove: IVP, 1979.
Editor: James E. Berney.
'The Living God is a Missionary God'.
See C(ii):1977, *Declare His Glory among the Nations*.

Zum Lebendigen Gott Bekehren
(Turn to the Living God)
Stuttgart: Evangelische Pfarramt der Ludwig-Hofacker-Gemeinde, 1979.
Editor: Winrich Scheffbuch.
Papers given at the Ludwig-Hofacker Conference, 1979.
'Die Bekehrung des Saulus von Tarsus'
(The Conversion of Saul of Tarsus).

1980

Believing and
Obeying Jesus Christ:
The Urbana '79
Compendium

Downers Grove: IVP, 1980.
Editor: James W. Alexander.
Addresses from the Inter-Varsity
missionary convention, Urbana, 1979.
'The Messenger and God: Studies in
Romans 1–5.'
i. 'God's Gospel'
ii. 'God's Judgment'
iii. 'God's Righteousness'
iv. 'God's People'

Proceedings of the
International
Conference of
Christian Medical
Students, 1980

London: ICCMS/Christian Medical
Fellowship, 1980.
Editor: Lee Moy Ng.
'The Whole Christian'.
i. 'Our Personal Integrity'
ii. 'Our Vocational Service'
iii. 'Our Social Responsibility'
iv. 'Our Ethical Distinctiveness'
v. 'Our Global Perspective'
See A:1986.

1981

Agenda for the
Biblical Church,
Vol. 2

Sydney: Anglican Information Office, 1981.
Editors: Alan Nichols and John W.
Williams.
'The Gospel and the Kingdom'.
An address at the Australian National
Evangelical Anglican Congress,
Melbourne, May 1981.

The Bible in
Perspective

London: The Bible Society, 1981.
The Olivier Beguin Lectures for 1975, 1976,
1978 and 1979.
'The Authority and Relevance of the Bible
in the Modern World'. See D(ii):1979;
C(ii):1984.

Faith Meets Faith

New York: Paulist Press/Grand Rapids:
Eerdmans, 1981.
Editors: Gerald H. Anderson and Thomas
F. Stransky.
'Dialogue, Encounter, even Confrontation'.
Reprinted from chapter 3 of *Christian
Mission in the Modern World*. See A:1975.

Let Every Tongue Confess	Downers Grove: IVP, 1981. Editors: Ken Shingledecker and James E. Berney. 'The Living God is a Missionary God'. See C(ii):1977, *Declare His Glory among the Nations*.
Perspectives on the World Christian Movement: A Reader	Pasadena: William Carey Library, 1981. Editors: Ralph D. Winter and Steven C. Hawthorne. 'The Bible in World Evangelization'. Adapted and condensed from an address at the Consultation on World Evangelization, Pattaya, Thailand, June 1980. 'The Living God is a Missionary God'. Adapted and condensed from an address at Urbana, 1976 (*cf. Declare His Glory among the Nations*, C(ii):1977) as reprinted in *You Can Tell the World*, C(ii):1979.

1983

'Bash': A Study in Spiritual Power	London: Marshalls, 1983. Editor: John Eddison. 'The Counsellor and Friend'. Revised edition, Crowborough: Highland Books, 1992 under the title *A Study in Spiritual Power*. See C(ii):1992.
Peacemakers: Christian Voices from the New Abolitionist Movement	New York: Harper & Row/Toronto: Fitzhenry & Whiteside, 1983. Editor: Jim Wallis. 'John R. W. Stott: an Anglican Clergyman'.

1984

The Bible in our World	Canberra: The Bible Society in Australia, 1984. The Olivier Beguin Lectures, 1974–1983. 'Scripture and Culture'. See D(ii):1979; C(ii):1981.
Faithful in Christ Jesus	Downers Grove: IVP, 1984. Editors: Bill Goheen and Karen Niedermayer. 'The Living God is a Missionary God'. See C(ii):1977, *Declare His Glory among the Nations*.

The Future of World Evangelization	Monrovia: Marc, 1984. Editors: Edward R. Dayton and Samuel Wilson. 'Ten Years Later: the Lausanne Covenant'.
Perspectives on Peacemaking	Ventura: Regal Books, 1984. Editor: John A. Bernbaum. 'Christian Responses to Good and Evil: A Study of Romans 12:9 – 13:10'.
Proclaiming Christ to His World	Oslo: Luther Forlag, 1984. Editors: Hanne-Grete Brommeland and Knud Jørgensen. A Festschrift in honour of Dr Sigurd Aske. 'Communication, Context and the Centrality of Jesus Christ'. See E(iii):Summer 1985.

1986

Hope for the Church of England?	Eastbourne: Kingsway, 1986. Editor: Gavin Reid. 'I Believe in the Church of England'.
Martyn Lloyd-Jones: Chosen by God	Crowborough: Highland Books, 1986. Editor: Christopher Catherwood. 'An Appreciation'.

1987

Should I not be Concerned?	Downers Grove: IVP, 1987. Editor: John E. Kyle. 'The Living God is a Missionary God'. See C(ii):1977, *Declare His Glory among the Nations*.
Stepping Stones: Joint Essays on Anglican Catholic and Evangelical Unity	London: Hodder & Stoughton, 1987. Editor: Christina Baxter. Consulting Editors: John Stott and Roger Greenacre. 'Mission Agenda for the People of God'. By James Robertson and John Stott. See B(ii):1987; C(i):1987.

1988

Christian Faith and Practice in the Modern World	Grand Rapids: Eerdmans, 1988. Editors: Mark A. Noll and David F. Wells. 'Biblical Meditation: True Wisdom'. 'Biblical Meditation: God in Christ'.

	'Biblical Meditation: The Restoration of Creation'.
Essentials:	London: Hodder and Stoughton, 1988.
A Liberal-Evangelical	By David L. Edwards and John Stott.
Dialogue	Published in the USA under the title *Evangelical Essentials*. See A:1988.
Handling Problems of	London: Marshall Pickering, 1988.
Peace and War	Editor: Andrew Kirk.
	'Nuclear Weapons Change the Possibility of War'.
	'Witnesses for the Defence: Reconciling Justice and Love'.

1989

Proclaiming Christ in	Oxford: Regnum Books, 1989.
Christ's Way:	Editors: Vinay Samuel and Albrecht
Studies in Integral	Hauser.
Evangelism	Essays presented to Walter Arnold on the occasion of his 60th birthday.
	'A Note about the Stuttgart Statement on Evangelism'.

1990

One Gospel – Many	Oxford: Evangelical Fellowship in the
Clothes	Anglican Communion and Regnum Books, 1990.
	Editors: Christopher Wright and Christopher Sugden.
	Published to mark the retirement of John Stott as President of the Evangelical Fellowship in the Anglican Communion.
	'Evangelism through the Local Church'.
	Reprinted as chapter 15 of *The Contemporary Christian*.
	See A:1992.
Proclaim Christ until	Minneapolis: World Wide Publications,
He Comes	1990.
	Editor: J. D. Douglas.
	The papers of Lausanne II, Manila, 1989.
	'Bible Studies on Romans 1–5'.
	'Eagerness to Preach the Gospel'
	'The World's Guilt'
	'Amazing Grace'

Sannheten Tro I
Kjærlighet
(Speaking the Truth
in Love)

See C(ii):1980, *Believing and Obeying Jesus Christ: The Urbana '79 Compendium*.
Oslo: Luther Forlag, 1990.
A Festschrift for Bishop Erling Utnem on his 70th birthday.
'Kristus og Misjonen: En Utfordring for Var Tid' (Christ and Mission: A Challenge for Today).
Revised and expanded as chapter 21 of *The Contemporary Christian*. See A:1992.

1991

For Christ and the University

Downers Grove: IVP, 1991.
By Keith and Gladys Hunt.
Appendix: 'Teacher and Lord' – a statement on the authority of Christ and the Scriptures given at the 1964 Inter-Varsity missionary convention. See *Decision*, E(iii): March 1965.

1992

Alive to God

Downers Grove: IVP, 1992.
Editors: J. I. Packer and Loren Wilkinson.
Studies in spirituality presented to James M. Houston.
'Pride, Humility and God'.

A Study in Spiritual Power

See C(ii):1983, *'Bash': A Study in Spiritual Power*.

1994

Vital Ministry Issues

Grand Rapids: Kregel, 1994.
Editor: Roy B. Zuck.
'The World's Challenge to the Church'.
'Ideals of Pastoral Ministry'.
See E(ii), *Bibliotheca Sacra* 1988–1989.

D: Booklets and Pamphlets

(i) Series

1962

The Episcopal series
1962

Atlanta: The Episcopal Radio-TV
Foundation, 1962.
A series of leaflets, the transcripts of radio
broadcasts for the Episcopal Radio-TV
Foundation, on the Apostles' Creed.
11 February *I Believe in God.*
18 February *Father and Creator.*
25 February *Jesus Christ, His Only Son.*
4 March   *Suffered under Pontius Pilate.*
11 March   *He Rose Again.*
18 March   *He Shall Come to Judge.*
25 March   *The Holy Spirit.*
1 April   *The Holy Catholic Church.*
8 April   *The Forgiveness of Sins.*
15 April   *The Resurrection and the Life
             Everlasting.*
See also E(ii): His 1968–1970, series on the
Apostles' Creed.

1964–1989

Chicago TV series

Chicago: Chicago Sunday Evening Club,
1964–1989.
A series of leaflets, the transcripts of TV
broadcasts for the Sunday Evening Club of
Chicago in the programme 'An Hour of
Good News', on Channel 11, WTTW,
Chicago, under the following titles:
1964 *Beginning a New Year With Christ.*
1972 *The Humility of a Little Child.*
1974 *Freedom Through Jesus Christ.*
1977 *Untitled Sermon Based on Matthew
      11:25–30.*
1978 *The Uniqueness of Jesus Christ.*
1979 *Christ Our Foundation.*
1980 *The Born Again Band Wagon.*
1981 *Work or Shirk.*
1982 *True Wisdom.*
1983 *An Appeal Which Cannot be Ignored.*
1984 *Not Christianity, but Christ.*

1985 *Jesus Christ is Risen Today!*
1986 *Glory in the Cross.*
1987 *Is There Any Hope?*
1989 *Relevance of the Resurrection.*

1979–1981

All Souls Papers   London: All Souls Church.
A series of leaflets containing sermons
delivered in All Souls on the dates given.
1979: 18 February   *Work and Unemployment.*
1979: 17 June   *Industrial Relations.*
Contained in the same paper as *Abortion.*
See below, 1 June 1980.
1979: 11 November *Calling for Peacemakers*
                                   in a Nuclear Age.
1980: 1 June   *Abortion.*
1981: 16 February   *The Christian and the*
                                   Poor.
See A:1984, *Issues Facing Christians Today.*

1985

'Contemporary   London: Marshalls and the London
Christian Issues'   Institute for Contemporary Christianity.
series   Three titles, all by John Stott, two booklets
and a book.
See B(i):1985; D(ii):1985.

(ii) Individual Titles

1949

Personal Evangelism   London: IVF, 1949.
Downers Grove: IVP, 1964.

1950

Becoming a Christian London: IVF, 1950.
Downers Grove: IVP, 1950.
Revised, 1972.

1952

Ezra the Scribe   London: The Berean Band, 1952.
Parochial Evangelism London: Church Information Board, 1952.
by the Laity   The substance of an address given to the
London Diocesan Conference, June 1952,
and subsequently expanded at the request

of the Standing Committee. As well as a number of re-printings, an enlarged edition was issued containing an Outline Training Syllabus. The booklet was also distributed by the Church Pastoral-Aid Society in their 'Fellowship Papers' series, June 1953.

1954

The Mind of Christ on Missions

London: China Inland Mission, n.d.
An address on John 4:31–38 given under the auspices of the China Inland Mission in Westminster Central Hall, 8 September 1953.

1955

Metaphorically Speaking – or The Complete Christian

London: Church Pastoral-Aid Society, 1955. No. 186 in the CPAS series of 'Fellowship Papers', March 1955.
Notes of an address given at the Whytham Camp, 7 August 1954, from 2 Timothy 2.

The Way to Heaven

London: Golders Green Crematorium, 1955.
An address given at the Service of Remembrance, 26 June 1955.

1956

Fundamentalism and Evangelism

London: Crusade Booklets, 1956. Reprinted and expanded from two articles in *Crusade*.
See E(iii):November 1955; E(iii): May 1956. For the USA edition, see A:1959.

The Lord's Prayer: A Christian Philosophy of Life

New York: WMGM Bible House, 1956. A radio address given on WMGM New York, 11 November 1956.

Why do the Innocent Suffer?

London: Crusade Booklets, 1956. An address in All Souls at a Service for Doctors, 16 October 1955, and published in *Crusade*, 1956.
See E(ii): All Souls Sermons 1946–1985; November 1955. Also E(iii): January 1956.

Why on Earth should I help the Jews?

London: Church Missions to Jews, 1956. The summary of an address in All Souls at the Church Missions to Jews Birthday Service.

1957

Being a Christian	London: IVF, 1957. Downers Grove: IVP, 1957. Incorporated as the final chapter of *Basic Christianity*. See A:1958.
The Ministry of St Paul (Parts 1 & 2)	London: Church Army Visual Aids Dept, 1957. Two booklets, CA13 and CA14, to accompany filmstrips.

1959

The Doctor – a Person	Cape Town: The Medical Christian Fellowship, Cape Town, 1959. The substance of a talk given at the Medical School, University of Cape Town, August 1959.

1961

Mobilizing the Church for Evangelism	London: All Souls Church, 1961. Notes to accompany a filmstrip.

1962

Motives and Methods in Evangelism	London: IVF, 1962. Downers Grove: IVP, 1967, slightly adapted, under the title *Evangelism: Why and How*. The substance of the Presidential Address at the Inter-Varsity Fellowship Annual Conference, April 1962.

1963

Beginning a New Life with Christ	London: Falcon, 1963. Five talks given on the BBC series 'Lift Up Your Hearts', December 1962 and January 1963. Revised 1974.
Intercommunion and Prayer Book Revision	London: Falcon, 1963. A reprint of three articles: from the *Church of England Newspaper* and from the *Church Times*. See E(iii): January 1962; E(iii): March 1963.

1964

The Baptism and Fullness of the Holy Spirit	London: IVF, 1964. Downers Grove: IVP, 1964 in book form: see A:1964. The substance of an address at the Islington Clerical Conference, January 1964, subsequently expanded. For the revised and enlarged edition see *Baptism and Fullness*, A:1975.
The Meaning of Evangelism	London: Falcon, 1964. Originally published as an article in *The Christian Graduate*, 1956. Revised, 1973. See E(iii): June 1956.
Personal Evangelism	Downers Grove: IVP, 1964. See D(ii):1949.

1967

An Appalling and Horrible Thing . . .	London: Church Pastoral-Aid Society, 1967. No. 255 in the CPAS series of 'Fellowship Papers', being the substance of the Annual Sermon of the Church Pastoral-Aid Society in All Souls, October 1966.
Evangelism: Why and How	Downers Grove: IVP, 1967. See D(ii):1962, *Motives and Methods in Evangelism*.

1968

The Call to Preach	London: London Baptist Preachers' Association, 1968. The Diamond Jubilee Lecture of the Association, in Bloomsbury Central Baptist Church, March 1968.

1971

Following Christ in the Seventies	Singapore: James Wong, 1971. Sydney: Anzea, 1972. The substance of a public lecture in Singapore, February 1971.

1972

The Bible and the Crisis of Authority	London: Falcon, 1972. The substance of the Annual Sermon of the British and Foreign Bible Society, 1972.

Divorce: The Biblical Teaching	London: Falcon, 1972. Originally published as an article in *The Churchman*, 1971. See E(iii): Autumn 1971. *Cf.* D(ii):1987, *Marriage and Divorce*.
Reverence for Human Life	London: Church Pastoral-Aid Society, 1972. The substance of an address in All Souls at a Service for Doctors, October 1971. Later published as two articles in the *Church of England Newspaper*, 1971; and here reprinted as No. 278 in the CPAS series of 'Fellowship Papers'. See E(iii): October 1971; E(iii) November 1971.
Your Mind Matters: The Place of the Mind in the Christian Life	London: IVF, 1972. Downers Grove: IVP, 1973 in book form. See A:1973. Reprinted, Brisbane: Australian Fellowship of Evangelical Students, 1994. The text of the Presidential Address at the Inter-Varsity Fellowship Annual Conference, 1972.

1974

The Authority of the Bible	Downers Grove: IVP, 1974. The substance of an address at the Inter-Varsity missionary convention, Urbana 1973, originally published in *Jesus Christ: Lord of the Universe, Hope of the World*. See C(ii):1974.
Salvation Yesterday and Today	Melbourne: Ridley College, 1974. The fourth Bishop Baker Memorial Lecture, and (simultaneously) the Tyndale Public Lecture, 30 April 1974; later expanded as chapter 4 of *Christian Mission in the Modern World*. See A:1975.

1975

Balanced Christianity	London: Hodder & Stoughton, 1975. Downers Grove: IVP, 1975.
Explaining the Lausanne Covenant	See immediately below.
The Lausanne Covenant: an Exposition and Commentary	Minneapolis: World Wide Publications, 1975 (also in book form: see A:1975). London: Scripture Union, 1975 under the title *Explaining the Lausanne Covenant*.

Reissued in the same year as 'Lausanne Occasional Paper, No. 3'.
See E(iii):January 1989.

Walk in His Shoes   London: IVP, 1975.
Downers Grove: IVP, 1976 under the title *Who is my Neighbor?*
Bombay: Gospel Literature Service, 1977. Produced in association with Tear Fund to accompany the sound strip of the same title.

1976

Who is my Neighbor?   Downers Grove: IVP, 1976.
See D(ii):1975, *Walk in His Shoes*.

1977

What is an Evangelical?   London: Falcon, 1977.
The closing address at the second National Evangelical Anglican Congress, Nottingham University, April 1977.

1978

Essentials for Tomorrow's Christians.   London: Scripture Union, 1978.
The text of the address in All Souls at the Evangelical Alliance President's Night, 1977.

1979

The Authority and Relevance of the Bible in the Modern World   Canberra: The Bible Society in Australia, 1979.
Downers Grove: IVP, 1981 under the title *Culture and the Bible*. The sixth Olivier Beguin Memorial Lecture, in Perth, Melbourne and Canberra, April and May, 1979. See C(ii):1981.

Calling for Peacemakers in a Nuclear Age   London: All Souls Papers, 1979.
The text of a sermon in All Souls, 11 November 1979.

1981

Culture and the Bible   See D(ii):1979, *The Authority and Relevance of the Bible in the Modern World*.

1982

Evangelical Anglicans and the ARCIC Final Report	Nottingham: Grove Books, 1982. An assessment and critique drafted by John Stott on behalf of the Church of England Evangelical Council: with a Foreword by John Stott and Timothy Dudley-Smith.

1983

In Christ: The Meaning and Implications of the Gospel of Jesus Christ	Washington: National Prayer Breakfast, 1983. The substance of an address at the Leadership Luncheon following the National Prayer Breakfast in Washington, D.C.
Make the Truth Known	Leicester: IVP, 1983. The Presidential Address to the British Isles Conference of the Universities and Colleges Christian Fellowship, 1982.

1985

Abortion	London: Marshalls and the London Institute for Contemporary Christianity, 1985. Chapter 15 from *Issues Facing Christians Today*. See A:1984; reprinted in the series 'Contemporary Christian Issues'. See B(i):1985.
A Call to Christian Leadership	London: Marshalls and the London Institute for Contemporary Christianity, 1985. Manila: Action International Ministries, 1987. Chapter 17 from *Issues Facing Christians Today*. See A:1984; reprinted in the series 'Contemporary Christian Issues'. See B(i):1985.

1987

Homosexual Partnerships?	Downers Grove: IVP, 1987. Adapted from chapter 8 in *Involvement*, *Vol.* 2, 1985. See A:1985.

Marriage and Divorce	Downers Grove: IVP, 1987. Adapted from chapter 6 in *Involvement*, *Vol. 2*, 1985. See A:1985.
Sermon on the Mount: Seeking First the Kingdom of God	London: Scripture Union, 1987. Downers Grove: IVP, 1991. Study Guide adapted from *Christian Counter-Culture: The Message of the Sermon on the Mount*. See A:1978.

1988

'What is the Spirit Saying . . .?'	Chippenham: Church of England Evangelical Council, 1988. The substance of the closing address at the National Evangelical Anglican Celebration, NEAC 3, April/May 1988, revised and enlarged to form a Report.

1989

God's Word for our Time	Sevenoaks: Hodder & Stoughton, 1989. Address at the New International Version tenth anniversary service, St Martin-in-the-Fields, 13 February 1989.
What is Man?	London: National Prayer Breakfast Committee, 1989. Address at the National Prayer Breakfast, 22 November 1989. See E(iii): January 1990/91.

1992

An Address by John Stott	Downers Grove: IVP, 1992. The address given at the International Tea in honour of John Stott during the Christian Booksellers Association Convention, Dallas, 28 June 1992.

1993

The Works of the Lord	Portimao, Portugal: A Rocha Trust, 1993. An address given at the tenth anniversary celebrations of the A Rocha Trust, a Christian Field Study Centre and Bird Observatory in the Algarve, South West Portugal, 25 September 1993.

(iii) As Editor, Part-Author or Contributor

1954

All Souls: An
Illustrated Guide
London: All Souls Church, 1954.
'The Church's Work' and 'The Church's
Message'.
See also D(iii):1980.

1955

The New Birth, the
New Status, the New
Walk
London: Church Pastoral-Aid Society, 1955.
No. 192 in the CPAS series of 'Fellowship
Papers'.
'The New Birth'. Reprinted from *Crusade*.
See E(iii): June 1955.

1956

Preparing for a Billy
Graham Crusade
New York: Billy Graham New York
Crusade, Inc., 1956.
'. . . Organize the Membership to Reach the
Unchurched'.

1963

Why I value the
North Side Position
London: Falcon, 1963.
Papers under this title by J. A. Motyer, A.
M. Stibbs and J. R. W. Stott; also issued as
No. 238 in the CPAS series of 'Fellowship
Papers'.

1967

Evening Prayer: A
Conservative
Translation into
Modern English
London: Falcon, 1967.
Text and introduction jointly by T. Dudley-
Smith, J. I. Packer and J. R. W. Stott, as
members of the Literature Committee of
the Evangelical Fellowship in the Anglican
Communion; also issued as No. 259 in the
CPAS series of 'Fellowship Papers' and as
an Order of Service for congregational use.

Keele '67 – the
National Evangelical
Anglican Congress
Statement
London: Falcon, 1967.
Editor: Philip Crowe.
'Introduction to the Statement'.

1977

| *Evangelism, Salvation and Social Justice* | Nottingham: Grove Books, 1977. By Ronald J. Sider with a response by John R. W. Stott. Ronald J. Sider's original article was published in the *International Review of Mission*, July 1975. John Stott's 'Response' was written for this booklet; and slightly revised for a second edition, 1979. |

1978

| *The Pasadena Consultation: Homogeneous Unit Principle* | Charlotte: Lausanne Committee for World Evangelization, 1978. Explanatory Preface by John Stott. Lausanne Occasional Paper No. 1. |

1980

| *All Souls Church, Langham Place, London* | London: All Souls Church, 1980. An illustrated history and guide, 'Window on the World'. See also D(iii):1954. |
| *An Evangelical Commitment to Simple Life-Style* | Wheaton: Lausanne Committee for World Evangelization, 1980. An Exposition and Commentary by Alan Nichols. 'Introduction' by John Stott and Ronald J. Sider. Lausanne Occasional Paper No. 20. |

1983

| *Be Angry and Sin Not* | London: Scripture Union, 1983. Editor: Myra Chave-Jones. A symposium jointly prepared from contributions by Dr Ruth Fowke, the Reverend Dick Keyes, and the Reverend J. R. W. Stott. 'Summary' by John Stott. |
| *Co-operating in World Evangelization* | Wheaton: Lausanne Committee for World Evangelization, 1983. 'Theological Preamble'. Lausanne Occasional Paper No. 24. |

1988

Towards a Renewed	Bramcote: Grove Books, 1988.
Church	Editors: Eric Kemp, Michael Harper and John Stott.
	A joint statement by Catholics, Charismatics and Evangelical Anglicans.

1994

Basic Christianity:	Downers Grove: IVP, 1994.
Six Studies for	With Dale and Sandy Larsen.
Individuals or Groups	Adapted from A:1958, *Basic Christianity*; C(ii):1971, *Christ the Liberator*.
The Church and the	Anaheim: Lutheran Bible Institute in
Moral Order	California, 1994.
	'Homosexual Partnerships' by John Stott. Reprinted from *Decisive Issues Facing Christians Today*.
	See A:1990.
God's Word for	Downers Grove: IVP, 1994.
Contemporary	With Scott Hotaling.
Christians:	Adapted from A:1992, *The Contemporary*
Six Studies for	*Christian*; A:1988, *Favourite Psalms*; A:1984,
Individuals or Groups	*The Message of 2 Timothy*; C(ii):1971, *Christ the Liberator*.

E: Contributions to Periodicals

(i) As Editor

1939–1940

THE METEOR 1939–1940 (Rugby School journal)

1939

October 16	Editorial
November 6	Editorial
November 27	Editorial
December 18	Editorial

1940

February 5	Editorial
March 4	Editorial
April 2	Editorial
May 27	Editorial
June 22	—
July 11	Editorial
July 29	Editorial

1947–1959

ALL SOULS (*monthly magazine of All Souls Church*)
Contributions by John Stott during this period will be found
listed in the two series of (a) sermons and (b) articles contributed
to *All Souls* from 1946 on. See E(ii):1946–1985 for sermons and
E(ii):1972–1991 for articles. John Stott began to edit the magazine
in 1947 during the illness of the Rector, the Revd Harold
Earnshaw-Smith, but took over as the regular editor from 1951 to
1959.

(ii) Series

1946–1985

ALL SOULS SERMONS *1946–1985.* The following are notes
or summaries of *sermons*, preached in St Peter's, Vere Street, or in
All Souls Church, Langham Place, London, unless otherwise
stated. For *articles* in the magazine over the same period see
under E(ii):1972–1991. No distinction is made here between the
magazine and the broadsheet which succeeded it in September/
October 1990.

1946

August	'A Stirring Invitation'	Psalm 95:1
	preached 20 January 1946.	
September	'Atheism'	Luke 12:20
	preached 21 July 1946.	
November	'The Heart in the Mouth'	Matthew 12:34
	preached 8 September 1946.	
1947		
April	'Life or Death?'	Revelation 3:1
	preached 9 February 1947.	
September	'The Initiative of God'	Genesis 1:1
	preached 3 August 1947.	
1948		
May	'Mutual Relationships'	Matthew 18:15–35
	preached 12 October 1947.	
June	'When He is Come'	John 16:8; 15:26;
	preached 25 April 1948.	16:13
July	'Pharisaism'	Mark 7:6–23
	preached 20 June 1948.	
August	'The Strategy of Satan'	Matthew 16:18;
	preached 11 July 1948.	Acts 5:39

November	'God's Truth through Man's Temperament' Notes of a series of addresses during September and October on the great writers of the New Testament. See A:1945 *Men with a Message*.	
1949		
March	'Growing Up' preached 16 January 1949.	1 Corinthians 3:1–3
June	'Christian Worship' preached 6 March 1949.	John 4:16, 23, 24
1950		
January	'Christ's Conquest of Man's Pride' Notes of a course of four sermons on Philippians beginning on 16 October 1949.	Philippians
February	'The Divine Burden Bearer' preached 8 January 1950.	Isaiah 40–64
March	'Christian Fellowship' preached at the lunch-hour Service 9 February 1950.	Philippians 1:3, 5
April	'In the Year that King Uzziah died . . .' preached 12 March 1950, on the death of the Rector.	Isaiah 6:1
May	'Christian Contentment' preached Easter Sunday 1950.	Philippians 4:11
June	'Conversion and Regeneration' preached 7 May 1950.	Matthew 18:3; John 3:5
July	'A Five Point Manifesto' preached 18 June 1950.	Acts 2:44
August	'The Limits of Christian Liberty' preached 9 July 1950.	Romans 4:14, 20
October	'Real Religion' preached 17 September 1950.	Galatians 6:15; 5:6; 1 Corinthians 7:19
December	'Remember the Spectators' preached 5 November 1950.	Hebrews 12:1–2
1951		
January	'On the Horizon' preached 3 December 1950.	Philippians 3:20, 21
February	'The Coming Judge' preached 10 December 1950	John 12:48
April	'Divine Teacher' preached 4 March 1951.	John 7:14–17
May	'Joy in Jerusalem' preached 15 April 1951.	Luke 24:52

July	'Hallelujah' preached 3 June 1951. See E(iii): September/October 1951.	Psalm 117:2
August	'It Pleased God' preached 17 June 1951.	Galatians 1:15, 16
September	'Seek and Ye Shall Find' preached at a broadcast Service, 22 July 1951.	Psalm 53:2

1952

January	'Election Manifesto' preached 21 October 1951.	1 Peter 2:17
February	'The Unity of the Church' preached 13 January 1952	John 17:20, 21
March	'God Save the Queen' preached 10 February 1952, the Sunday after the Queen's Accession.	Joshua 1:15
April	'Divine Love' preached 24 February 1952.	John 3:16
June	'The Saviour of the World' preached 21 May 1952.	Luke 24:46–51
July	'The New Covenant' preached 8 June 1952.	Jeremiah 31:31–44
August	'The Ten Commandments' preached 22 June 1952.	Exodus 20
November	'True Health' preached 19 October 1952 at a Service for Doctors.	1 Thessalonians 5:23
December	'The Inheritance of the Saints' preached 2 November 1952.	Revelation 7

1953

January	'Priesthood and Sacrifice' preached 14 December 1952.	Hebrews 7:23–27
March	'The Sabbath and Man' preached 25 January 1953.	Mark 2:27
April	'What Jesus Taught about God' preached 22 February 1953.	Matthew 6:9–10
May	'The Christian Life' preached 22 March 1953.	Mark 8:34–35
June	'Who is He that Condemneth?' preached 17 May 1953.	Romans 8:34
July	'Modern Jonahs' preached 21 June 1953.	Psalm 139:9–10
October	'The Steadfast Love of God' preached 6 September 1953.	Psalm 36:7–9
November	'Christian Workers' preached 20 September 1953.	2 Timothy 2

December	'The Human Body' preached 18 October 1953 at a Service for Doctors. See E(iii):February 1954.	1 Corinthians 6: 19, 20
1954		
January	'Jesus Christ and the Bible' preached 6 December 1953.	John 5:39, 40
February	'Epiphany' preached 10 January 1954.	Titus 2:11–13
March	'Weeds and Wheat' preached 7 February 1954.	Matthew 13:24–30, 36–43
April	'Compassion' preached 28 February 1954.	Mark 6:34
May	'The Things Concerning Jesus' preached Easter Day 1954.	Luke 24:19–27
July	'The Exaltation of Jesus' preached 30 May 1954.	Philippians 2:9–11
August	'Spiritual Depression' preached 4 July 1954.	Psalm 42:5, 11; 43:5
September	'Christ's Programme' preached at a televised Family Service, 27 June 1954.	Acts 1:8
November	'The Nature of Man' preached 18 October 1954 at a Service for Doctors.	Psalm 8:3–6
December	'Christian Education' preached 24 October 1954.	1 Timothy 6:2–5
1955		
January	'The Christian Hope' preached 28 November 1954.	Revelation 22: 20, 21
February	'Truth and Love' preached 2 January 1955.	1 Corinthians 3:1–3
March	'Silence' preached 23 January 1955.	Habakkuk 2:20
April	'The Obedience of Faith' preached 6 March 1955.	Hebrews 11:8
June	'Go and Tell' preached 20 March 1955.	Mark 5:18–20
July	'A Child's Humility' preached 1 May 1955 before the University of Cambridge, and 8 May 1955 in All Souls. See E(iii):May 1955.	Matthew 18:1–4
August	'The Trinity' preached 12 June 1955.	Matthew 6:7–13
October	'The Holy Spirit and the Bible' preached 4 September 1955.	1 Corinthians 2:9–14

November	'Attitudes to Suffering' preached 16 October 1955 at a Service for Doctors See D(ii): 1956, *Why do the Innocent* *Suffer?*	The Book of Job
December	'Rock of Ages' preached 12 June 1955.	Psalm 27:5
1956		
January	'That Day' preached 27 November 1955.	2 Thessalonians 1:7–10
February	'Christian Joy' preached 8 January 1956.	Psalm 32:10, 11
April	'Questions Jesus Asked' preached 8 January 1956.	Mark 10:51; John 5:6; Matthew 9:28
May	'Why did Christ Die?' preached 25 March 1956.	Matthew 21–27
June	'Incentives to Work' preached 29 April 1956.	Colossians 3:23
July	'Relationships' preached 3 June 1956.	Colossians 3:17, 23
August	'What think Ye of Christ?' preached 10 June 1956.	1 Timothy 2:3–6
September	'Full Assurance of Faith' preached 15 July 1956.	Hebrews 10:19, 22
October	'The Supremacy of Love' preached 26 August 1956.	Luke 10:26, 27
November	'Luke the Physician' preached 14 October 1956 at a Service for Doctors.	Luke 3:6
December	'God's Glory and Grace' preached 28 October 1956.	Matthew 6:9–15
1957		
April	'New Individuals' preached 17 March 1957 at a broadcast Service.	2 Corinthians 5:17
May	'Justification and Sanctification' preached 16 September 1956	1 Timothy 1:15
June	'The Resurrection of the Body, 1' preached 12 May 1957.	1 Corinthians 15:35
July	'The Resurrection of the Body, 2' preached 19 May 1957.	1 Corinthians 15:43, 44
October	'What God Desires' preached 1 September 1957.	Hosea 6:6
November	'Christian Giving' preached 22 September 1957.	2 Corinthians 8:3
December	'The Sickness of Man' preached 20 October 1957 at a Service for Doctors.	Mark 2:17

1958

January	'Our Lord's Appearing' preached 1 December 1957.	1 John 3:1–13
February	'Snobbery' preached 5 January 1958.	Matthew 2:1
March	'A Humble Minister' preached 15 December 1957.	John 3:25–30
April	'Jubilate Deo' preached 9 March 1958.	Psalm 100
June	'Friend of Publicans and Sinners' preached 27 April 1958.	Luke 15:1, 2
October	'Be Strong and of Good Courage' preached 7 September 1958.	Deuteronomy 31: 6–8
November	'The Servant of the Lord' preached 21 September 1958.	Isaiah 42:1–4
December	'The Scientific Method' preached 10 October 1958 at a Service for Doctors.	John 20:25

1959

January	'A Teacher Come from God' preached 19 October 1958.	John 3:1, 2
February	'Christ and the Scriptures' preached 7 December 1958.	John 5:39, 40
March	'Justification by Faith' preached 25 January 1959.	Galatians 2:16
April	'He is Risen' preached during Lent 1959.	Matthew 28:6

Note: The date 1956 in *All Souls* attached to the sermon for April is surely a
misprint, since Lent 1959 saw a series of addresses on the Creed.

May	'Seated at the Right Hand of God' preached 12 April 1959.	Hebrews 1:3
June	'The Activity of the Holy Spirit' preached 17 May 1959.	2 Peter 1:21; 1 Peter 1:11
August	'God the Creator and Sustainer' preached 22 February 1959.	from the Creed
November	'Church or Bible?' preached 27 September 1959.	Article XX
December	'The Doctor as a Person' preached 18 October 1959 at a Service for Doctors.	Colossians 3:23

1960

January	'Rekindling the Inner Fire' preached 22 November 1959.	2 Timothy 1:6, 7
February	'If Thy Brother Sin against Thee' preached 17 January 1960.	Matthew 18:15–17
March	'A Study of Revival' preached 3 January 1960.	2 Chronicles 7:1–3

April	'Amos, Prophet of God's Justice' preached 6 March 1960.	Amos 5:24
May	'Isaiah, Prophet of God's Sovereignty' preached 20 March 1960.	Isaiah 6:5
July	'The Promise is to You' preached 5 June 1960.	Acts 2:38, 39
August	'Truth and Love' preached 3 July 1960.	2 John 1–3
September	'The Christian Conflict' preached 24 July 1960.	James 4:7, 8
October	'A Clear Conscience' preached 11 September 1960.	Acts 24:16
November	'The Miracles of Jesus' preached 16 October 1960 at a Service for Doctors.	John 20:30, 31
December	'Incentives in Evangelism' preached 6 November 1960.	Romans 1:15
1961		
January	'Living in the New Age' preached 27 November 1960.	1 Thessalonians 5:4–8
February	'To the Praise of His Glory' preached 15 January 1961 in the Chapel Royal.	Ephesians 1:6, 12, 14
March	'Waiting upon God' preached 22 January 1961.	Isaiah 40:31
April	'Why Weepest Thou?' preached Easter Day 1960.	John 20:11, 15
May	'The Jealousy of God' preached 26 February 1961.	Exodus 34:14
June	'The Doctrine of the Trinity' preached 12 June 1960.	Luke 11:3, 4
July	'The Fruit of the Spirit' preached 21 May 1961.	Galatians 5:22, 23
August	'The Confession of Sin' preached 2 July 1961.	Proverbs 28:13
September	'Preparing for Persecution' preached 23 July 1961.	Acts 4:29
October	'Lessons from the Weather' preached 4 October 1959.	Matthew 5:45
November	'The Lord's Servant' preached 17 September 1961.	Isaiah 50:4–7
December	'Childlikeness' preached 22 October 1961 at a Service for Doctors.	Matthew 18:1–4
1962		
January	'When He Appears' preached 3 December 1961.	1 John 2:28

February	'The Eyes of the Lord' preached 7 January 1962.	2 Chronicles 16:9
March	'The Joy of Jerusalem' preached 28 January 1962.	Nehemiah 12:43
April	'The Power of God' preached 2 April 1961.	Ephesians 1:18–22
May	'True Heart-Worship' preached 1 April 1962.	Mark 7:6, 7
July	'Authority – Scripture or Tradition?' preached 11 March 1962.	Mark 7:7, 8
August	'This Man Receiveth Sinners' preached 8 July 1962.	Luke 15:1, 2
September	'The Strategy of Satan' preached 5 August 1962.	2 Corinthians 2:11
October	'The Heavenly Potter' preached 2 September 1962.	Jeremiah 18:6
November	'The Paroxysm of Paul' preached 23 September 1962.	Acts 17:16, 17
December	'Motives in Medicine' preached 21 October 1962 at a Service for Doctors.	Matthew 9:35, 36

1963

January	'Christian Faith' preached 4 November 1962.	Hebrews 11:1, 2
February	'Man's Response to God's Word' preached 9 December 1962.	Psalm 119:161–163
March	'Trust and Obey' preached 6 January 1963.	1 Chronicles 10: 13, 14
April	'The Divine Wrestler' preached 3 February 1963.	Genesis 32:24–26
May	'The Little Flock of Jesus' preached 31 March 1963.	Luke 12:32
June	'The Eyes of the Heart' preached 5 May 1963.	Ephesians 1:17–19
July	'The Greater Ministry of the Spirit' preached 2 June 1963.	John 16:7
August	'Honest to God' preached 9 June 1963.	1 Timothy 2:5, 6
September	'The Heavenly Voice' preached 4 August 1963.	Matthew 17:5
November	'Christian Priorities' preached 4 October 1963.	1 Peter 4:7–11
December	'The Christian Perspective on Death' preached 20 October 1963 at a Service for Doctors.	1 Corinthians 15:26

1964

January	'An Exhortation to Christians' preached 22 September 1963.	1 Corinthians 15:58
February	'The Spirits of Just Men made Perfect' preached 3 November 1963.	Hebrews 12:22–24
March	'The Wide-Open Mouth' preached 5 January 1964.	Psalm 81:10, 11
April	'Following Jesus' preached 9 February 1964.	1 Peter 2:21
May	'The Cross and the Forgiveness of Sins' preached 1 March 1964.	Ephesians 1:7, 8
June	'The Cross and the Resurrection' preached 29 March 1964.	1 Corinthians 15: 3–5
July	'The Wise Man's Tongue and Ears' preached 19 April 1964.	Proverbs 12:15, 18
August	'Loving Christ' preached 21 June 1964.	John 14:21
September	'Baptism and Salvation' preached 19 July 1964.	Acts 2:38
October	'Ambitions in Contrast' preached 26 July 1964.	Mark 10:43
November	'Saul Turned Paul' preached 13 September 1964.	Philippians 3:3
December	'Physician Heal Yourself' preached 18 October 1964 at a Service for Doctors.	Luke 4:23

1965

January	'The Throne of Grace' preached 15 November 1964.	Hebrews 4:14–16
February	'Christlikeness' preached 29 November 1964.	1 John 3:2
April	'Man by Nature' preached 21 February 1965.	Ephesians 2:1–3
May	'The Nature of the Church' preached 14 March 1965.	1 Peter 2:9, 10
June	'The Great Commission' preached 4 April 1965.	Luke 24:46–49
July	'Patient Continuance in Well-Doing' preached 16 May 1965.	Romans 2:6, 7
August	'God is my Witness' preached 9 May 1965	1 Thessalonians 2:5; Romans 1:9; Philippians 1:8
September	'Listen to Christ!' preached 1 August 1965.	Mark 9:2, 7
October	'Obsession with Sin' preached 15 August 1965.	Romans 6:23

November	'The Justification of Man' preached 26 September 1965 at a broadcast Service.	Articles XI and XII
December	'The Good Samaritan' preached 17 October 1965 at a Service for Doctors.	Luke 10:25–37
1966		
January	'No Cause for Alarm' preached 14 November 1965.	Matthew 24:6–8
February	'A Christian's Priorities' preached 2 January 1966.	2 Corinthians 4:5
March	'Freedom in Christ' preached 23 January 1966.	Galatians 3:26–29
April	'The Invisible God' preached 30 January 1966.	John 1:18; 1 John 4:12
May	'The Doing of God's Will' preached 20 March 1966.	Matthew 6:10
June	'The Doxology' preached 24 April 1966.	Matthew 6:13
July	'The Ascension of Jesus Christ' preached 22 May 1966.	John 20:17
August	'Christian Conversion' preached 26 June 1966.	Acts 9
September	'The Stumbling Block of the Cross' preached 24 July 1966 at a broadcast Service.	1 Corinthians 1:23
November	'Article XXVII: Of Baptism' preached 22 September 1960.	Article XXVII
December	'The Psychosomatic Principle' preached 9 October 1966 at a Service for Doctors.	Proverbs 14:30; 17:22
1967		
January	'Man's Earthly Paradise' preached 20 November 1966.	Genesis 2:4–17
February	'The Biblical Doctrine of Marriage' preached 27 November 1966.	Genesis 2:18
March	'The Tragic Story of Cain' preached 15 January 1967.	Genesis 4:1–16
April	'From Adam to Noah' preached 5 February 1967.	Genesis 5
May	'Jesus the Word' preached 26 February 1967.	John 1:1–5, 14
June	'The Tower of Babel' preached 23 April 1967.	Genesis 10 & 11
July	'The Ministry of the Holy Spirit' preached Whit Sunday 1967.	John 14–16
November	'A Good and Faithful Servant' preached 17 September 1967.	1 Samuel 12:22, 23

December	'The Lord our Physician' preached 8 October 1967 at a Service for Doctors.	Exodus 15:26
1968		
January	'Paul's Final Charge' preached 3 December 1967.	2 Timothy 4:1–8
February	'Such a Great Salvation' preached 10 December 1967.	Hebrews 2:3
April	'Jesus Christ and Morality' preached 18 February 1968.	Matthew 4:10, 11
May	'God in His World' preached 3 March 1968.	Psalm 115:2, 3
June	'God in the Christian' preached 7 April 1968.	Romans 8:9–12
July	'Church and Nation' preached 26 May 1968.	Proverbs 13:34
September	'The Biblical Ideal of Newness' preached 21 July 1968.	2 Corinthians 5:17
October	'The Christian Ministry' preached 21 July 1968.	Ephesians 4:11, 12
November	'The Call to Die' preached 15 September 1968.	Luke 9:23, 24
December	'A Christian Philosophy of Life and Death' preached 13 October 1968 at a Service for Doctors.	Philippians 1:21
1969		
January	'Peacemakers' preached 10 November 1968.	Matthew 5:9
February	'Salvation – Merit or Mercy?' preached 24 November 1968.	Luke 18:9–14
March	'Worship – Lips or Heart?' preached 19 January 1969.	Mark 7:6, 7
April	'We are God's Children Now' preached 23 February 1969.	1 John 3:1, 2
May	'Your Father Knows' preached 9 March 1969.	Matthew 6:31–33
September	'Christ's Easy Yoke' preached 3 August 1969.	Matthew 11:28–30
October	'Christian Joy and Sorrow' preached 17 August 1969.	2 Corinthians 6:10
November	'The Spirit's Message to the Church' preached 7 September 1969.	Revelation 2:7
December	'Ambition – False or True?' preached 12 October 1969 at a Service for Doctors.	Jeremiah 9:23, 24

1970

February	'On Not Anticipating the Judgement' preached 14 December 1969.	1 Corinthians 4:5
March	'The Unsearchable Riches of Christ' preached 11 January 1970.	Ephesians 3:8
April	'Advice to a Young Leader' preached 25 January 1970.	1 Timothy 4:11, 12
May	'Genuine Peace' preached 15 March 1970.	Acts 10:36
June	'Solemn Charge to a Man of God' preached 26 April 1970.	1 Timothy 6:11–16, 20, 21
August	'Aliens in a Foreign Land' preached 7 June 1970 at a broadcast Service.	1 Peter 2:11
September	'The Christian Watchman' preached 12 July 1970.	(topical)
October	'Fasting and the Christian' preached 23 August 1970.	(topical)
November	'Christian Maturity' preached 20 September 1970.	Colossians 1:28, 29
December	'The Doctor, Humanist or Christian?' preached 11 October 1970 at a Service for Doctors.	Acts 20:35

1971

January	'The Two Ways' preached 15 November 1970.	Matthew 7:13, 14
March	'Encouragement to Pray' preached 8 November 1970.	Matthew 7:7–11
May	'Freedom from Fear' preached 29 March 1971.	Romans 8:15
July	'The Significance of Pentecost for the World' preached 2 May 1971.	Acts 2
September	'Peace through Pain' preached 13 June 1971.	Galatians 5:22
November	'The Anglican Doctrine of Holy Communion' preached 26 September 1971.	Articles XXVIII and XXIX

1972

February	'The Faith of Abraham' preached 2 January 1972.	Genesis 12:1–3
April	'The Tongue of the Wise' preached 20 February 1972.	Proverbs 12:15–19
June	'The Commission of the Risen Lord' preached Easter Day 1972.	John 20:19–23

August	'The Doctrine of the Trinity' preached 28 May 1972.	John 14:15–18
November	'The Fellowship of the Spirit' preached 4 June 1972.	Philippians 2:1–5
1973		
January	'The Fruit of the Spirit' preached 25 June 1972.	Galatians 5:22, 23
March	'We love . . .' preached 1 January 1973.	1 John 4:10–12
May	'Employer and Employee' preached 28 January 1973.	Colossians 3:22 – 4:1
July	'The Prisoner of the Lord' preached 1 April 1973.	Acts 28:30, 31
September	'The Responsibility to Grow' preached 29 July 1973.	1 Peter 2:1–3
November	'Salvation Today' preached 7 October 1973.	Romans 1:16
1974		
April	'Global Vision' preached 3 March 1974.	(topical)
June	'Watch and Pray' preached 7 April 1974.	Luke 22:46
August	'All for the Sake of the Gospel' preached 30 June 1974.	1 Corinthians 9:23
October	'The Holy Spirit in Evangelism' preached 25 August 1974.	1 Corinthians 2:3–5
December	'The Mystery and Mastery of Suffering' preached 6 October 1974 at a Service for Doctors.	Psalm 22
1975		
January/ February	'I Have a Dream . . . delivered 24 November 1974 at the 150th anniversary of All Souls church.	(topical)
April/May	'Be What You Are' preached 2 March 1975.	Ephesians 5:3–21
May/June	'Spiritual Weapons for Spiritual Warfare' preached 23 March 1975.	Ephesians 6:10–24
September/ October	'The Balance of the Bible' preached 4 May 1975.	1 Peter 2:1–13
December	'The Whereabouts of God' preached 12 October 1975 at a Service for Doctors.	Psalm 79:10; 42:3
1976		
March	'Beware of Covetousness' preached 14 December 1975.	Exodus 20:17

June	'Sent into the World' preached 28 March 1976.	John 17:18; 20:21
September/October	'Faith and the Knowledge of God' preached 23 May 1976.	Isaiah 40
December	'Jesus Christ Pre-eminent' preached 2 November 1976 at the re-opening of All Souls.	Colossians 1:18

1977

June	'Great God of History' preached 6, 13, 20 and 27 March and 2 April 1977.	Romans 9–11
October/November	'How Can a Man Know God?' preached 24 July 1977.	Psalm 19

1978

July/August	'The Ascension of Jesus Christ' preached 30 April 1978.	Hebrews 10:11–13

1979

July/August	'Justified by Faith'	Romans 5:1
	'Peace with God'	Romans 5:1
	'Standing in Grace'	Romans 5:2
	'Rejoicing in Hope' a summary of four sermons preached in Lent 1979.	Romans 5:2

1980

January/February	'Life, Death and Resurrection' preached 18 November 1979 at a Service for Doctors.	1 Corinthians 15:26

1981

Nil

1982

January/February	'A Biblical Definition of Health' preached 15 November 1981.	Job 28:28
September/October	'Daily Grace' preached in the summer of 1982.	Lamentations 3:17–23

1983

September/October	'Cross Purposes' preached 24 July 1983.	Romans 5–8

1984

January/February	'The Whereabouts of God' preached 20 November 1983 at a Medical Service.	Psalm 139:1–10
September/October	'The Verdict on Christ Reversed' preached 22 July 1984.	Acts 4:2; 17:18
November/December	'The Virgin Birth of Jesus' preached 7 October 1984.	Luke 1:26ff

1985

September/	'A Christian Mind on Feminism:	
October	1. The Equality of the Sexes'	Galatians 3:28
	preached 16 June 1985.	
November/	'A Christian Mind on Feminism:	
December	2. The Complementarity of the Sexes'	Genesis 2:18
	preached 16 June 1985.	

See also E(iii):September/October 1989.

1958

LIFE OF FAITH 1958 'The Gospel in the Canticles'

April 10	1. 'The Venite: The People of Salvation'	Psalm 95
April 17	2. 'Benedictus: The Context of Salvation'	Luke 1:67–69
April 24	3. 'Jubilate Deo: The Joy of Salvation'	Psalm 100
May 1	4. 'The Magnificat: The Condition of Salvation'	Luke 1:46–55
May 8	5. 'Deus Misereatur: The Knowledge of Salvation'	Psalm 67
May 22	6. 'Nunc Dimittis: The Results of Salvation'	Luke 2:29–32

See A:1966, *The Canticles and Selected Psalms*.

NURSING MIRROR 1958 Series for Advent

December 5	1. 'Christmas – the Answer to Fear'
December 12	2. 'Christmas – the Conquest of Pride'
December 19	3. 'Christmas – and Salvation'
December 26	4. 'Christmas – and the Conquest of Selfishness'

1962

LIFE OF FAITH 1962 'The First Century Christian Church: studies in 1 Corinthians 1–6.' Bible Readings from the Keswick Convention, 1962.

July 19	1. 'The First Century Christian Church: Its Unity'	1 Corinthians 1: 1–17
July 28	2. 'The First Century Christian Church: Its Humility'	1 Corinthians 1:18 – 3:4
August 3	3. 'The First Century Christian Church: Its Ministry'	1 Corinthians 3:5 – 4:21
August 23	4. 'The First Century Christian Church: Its Purity' (Pt. I)	1 Corinthians 5
August 30	5. 'The First Century Christian Church: Its Purity' (Pt. II)	1 Corinthians 6

See C(ii):1962.

1963–1964

LIFE OF FAITH 1963–1964 'Corinthian Controversy: Studies in 1 Corinthians 7–16'

1963

October 17	1.'Christian Marriage'	1 Corinthians 7:1–9
October 24	2. 'Divorce, Celibacy and Widowhood'	1 Corinthians 7: 10–40
October 31	3. 'Christian Liberty'	1 Corinthians 8
November 7	4. 'Apostolic Example'	1 Corinthians 9
November 14	5. 'Church Membership'	1 Corinthians 10
November 21	6. 'Church Worship'	1 Corinthians 11
November 28	7. 'Spiritual Gifts'	1 Corinthians 12: 1–13
December 5	8. 'The Diversity of Spiritual Gifts'	1 Corinthians 12:14–31
December 12	9. 'St Paul's Hymn of Love'	1 Corinthians 13: 1–3
December 19	10. 'Essential Qualities of Christian Love'	1 Corinthians 13: 4–13
December 26	11. 'Tongues and Prophecy'	1 Corinthians 14: 1–12

1964

January 2	12. 'Tongues and their Interpretation'	1 Corinthians14: 13–25
January 9	13. 'Tongues and Prophecy Controlled'	1 Corinthians 14: 26–40
January 16	14. 'Christ's Resurrection and Ours'	1 Corinthians 15: 1–34
January 23	15. 'The Mode of Resurrection'	1 Corinthians 15: 35–50
January 30	16. 'Christian Giving'	1 Corinthians 16: 1–4
February 13	17. 'Christian Hospitality'	1 Corinthians 16: 5–12
February 20	18. 'Apostolic Exhortations'	1 Corinthians 16: 13–24

Note: The serial number 18 attached to the article for 20 February is given in error as 19 in *Life of Faith*.

1965

IN THE SERVICE OF MEDICINE 1965 'Studies in 1 Corinthians'. Extracts from Bible Studies given at the Christian Medical Fellowship Conference, Bournemouth, May 1964.

January	'Love and Knowledge'	1 Corinthians 8
April	'Paul's View of the Body'	1 Corinthians 6: 9–20

| July | 'Diversity of Members – One Body' | 1 Corinthians 12: 14–31 |

LIFE OF FAITH 1965 'Studies in Paul's Second Letter to the Corinthians'

March 4	1. 'Marks of Christian Ministry'	2 Corinthians 1: 1–11
March 11	2. 'Letters and Visits to Corinth'	2 Corinthians 1:12 – 2:4
March 18	3. 'Frustration and Triumph'	2 Corinthians 2: 5–17
March 25	4. 'Letters Testimonial'	2 Corinthians 3: 1–12
April 1	5. 'Problems of Christian Ministry'	2 Corinthians 3:12 – 4:2
April 8	6. 'Hard Hearts and Blind Minds'	2 Corinthians 4:1–6
April 15	7. 'Weakness in Christian Ministry'	2 Corinthians 4: 7–18
April 22	8. 'Motives in Christian Ministry'	2 Corinthians 5: 11–17
April 29	9. 'The Body, Old and New'	2 Corinthians 5:1–10
May 13	10. 'Our Message'	2 Corinthians 5: 18–21
October 7	11. 'Duty and Heartache'	2 Corinthians 6:1–7
October 14	12. 'Criticisms which Confront the Christian'	2 Corinthians 6: 8–10
October 21	13.'Christian Life and its Detractors'	2 Corinthians 6:11 – 7:16
October 28	14. 'Grace and Giving'	2 Corinthians 8:1–5
November 4	15. 'Gracious Giving: The Will and the Deed'	2 Corinthians 8: 6–21
November 11	16. 'Christian Giving: Sowing and Reaping'	2 Corinthians 8:22 – 9:14
November 18	17. 'Detractors and Deceivers'	2 Corinthians 10:1 – 11:21
November 25	18. 'Paul's Defence of his Apostleship'	2 Corinthians 10: 1–12
December 2	19. 'Paul's Evangelistic Zeal'	2 Corinthians 10:13 – 11:15
December 9	20.'Paul's Apostolic Sufferings'	2 Corinthians 11: 16–33
December 16	21. 'Power and Authority'	2 Corinthians 12: 1–10
December 23	22. 'Paul's Concluding Admonitions'	2 Corinthians 12: 11–18
December 30	23. 'Paul's Concluding Exhortations'	2 Corinthians 12:19 – 13:14

Note: The serial number 20, attached to the article for 9 December, is given in error as 19 in *Life of Faith*. Similarly for serial numbers 21, 22, 23.

1965–1966

CRUSADE *1965–1966* 'Sit down with your Bible'. Taken from *The Canticles and Selected Psalms*. See A:1966.

1965

October	'Psalm 22'
November	'Psalm 40'
December	'Psalm 51'

1966

January	'Psalms 121, 122, 123'
February	'Psalm 150'

1966–1980

CHURCH HERALD (USA) *1966–1980*. The following is a series of articles contributed irregularly over this period, in most instances reproduced from the magazine *All Souls*. Where a date appears in brackets after an entry, this refers to the date of issue of *All Souls* from which the article (or, more usually, sermon) has been reproduced or adapted, not always with the same title. See E(ii):All Souls Sermons 1946–1985; E(ii):All Souls Articles 1972–1991.

1966

April 8	'Why Weepest Thou?' (April 1961)

1967

September 29	'The Stumbling Block of the Cross' (September 1966)

1968

May 17	'The Ascension of Jesus Christ' (July 1966)
September 6	'Uppsala: an Evangelical Assessment'
November 29	'The Psycho-somatic Principle' (December 1966)

1969

March 28	'The Call to Die' (November 1968)
May 23	'The Ministry of the Holy Spirit' (July 1967)
June 6	'Christian Conversion' (August 1966)
June 27	'The Church and the Nation' (July 1968)
September 5	'How May I Know the Will of God?' (May 1966)

1970

February 6	'Jesus Christ and Morality' (April 1968)
March 25	'Easter Myth or Easter Truth?'
	Reprinted from *Inter-Varsity*, October 1967.
	See E(iii): October 1967.
May 15	'God in the Christian' (June 1968)
May 22	'The Christian Ministry' (October 1968)

1971

January 8	'A Christian Philosophy of Life and Death' (December 1968)

March 26   'Genuine Peace' (May 1970)
April 23   'Humanist or Christian: Which?' (December 1970)
June 4   'God is not Silent' (November 1969)
September 24   'Aliens in a Foreign Land' (August 1970)
1972
April 14   'Peace through Pain' (September 1971)
April 28   'The Two Ways' (January 1971)
May 19   'The Significance of Pentecost for the World' (July 1971)
June 9   'The Biblical Ideal of Newness' (September 1968)
July 14   'Encouragement to Pray' (March 1971)
September 8   'Christ's Easy Yoke' (September 1969)
November 24   'Freedom from Fear' (May 1971)
December 22   'And the Word became Flesh (May 1967)
1973
April 20   'The Commission of the Risen Lord' (June 1972)
May 18   'Solemn Charge to a Man of God' (June 1970)
July 13   'Authority and Freedom' (April 1973)
               See E(ii):All Souls Articles 1972–1991; April 1973.
August 24   'Labor Relations According to St. Paul' (May 1973)
September 21   'Jesus Christ is the Answer' (March 1970)
October 5   'We Love' (March 1973)
1974
May 31   'The Fruit of the Spirit' (January 1973)
August 9   'Getting our Priorities Right'
               See E(ii):All Souls Articles 1972–1991; February 1974.
October 4   'Salvation Today' (November 1973)
1975
January 10   'Christian Joy and Sorrow' (October 1969)
March 7   'Saving and Serving'
               Adapted from an address, 'The Biblical Basis of
               Evangelism' given at the International Congress on
               World Evangelization, Lausanne, July 1974. See
               C(ii):1975, *Let the Earth hear His Voice.*
March 16   'Biblical Evangelism' (a continuation of the article above)
December 5   'The Mystery and Mastery of Suffering' (December 1974)
1976
January 23   'The Balance of the Bible' (September/October 1975)
February 20   'What's the State of the Gospel?'
               See E(iv):1976.
August 6   'Be What You Are' (April/May 1975)
December 10   'Go Therefore and Make Disciples of All Nations'
               See C(ii):1977, 'The Biblical Basis for Declaring God's
               Glory' in *Declare His Glory among the Nations.*
1980
February 22   'The Christian Watchman' (September 1970)
August 8   'Jesus' Teaching about the Trinity' (August 1972)

1967–1968

CRUSADE *1967–1968* 'But the Bible says . . .'

1967

September	'. . . about Sin' Reprinted from *All Souls*, October 1965.	Romans 6:23
October	'. . . about the Cross and Forgiveness' Reprinted from *All Souls*, May 1964.	Ephesians 1:7, 8
November	'. . . about Justification' Reprinted from *All Souls*, November 1965.	Ephesians 2:8
December	'. . . about Baptism and Salvation' Reprinted from *All Souls*, September 1964.	Acts 2:38

1968

January	'. . . about the Church' Reprinted from *All Souls*, May 1965.	1 Peter 2:9, 10
March	'. . . about Marriage' Reprinted from *All Souls*, February 1967.	Genesis 2:18

See E(ii):All Souls Sermons 1946–85 for dates shown.

1968

CHRISTIANITY TODAY (USA) *1968* 'The Great Commission'

April 26	'The Great Commission 1.'
May 10	'The Great Commission 2.'
May 24	'The Great Commission 3.'

See C(ii):1967, *One Race, One Gospel, One Task*.

1968–1970

HIS (USA) *1968–1970 The Apostles' Creed*. Adapted from the series of radio broadcasts given for the Episcopal Radio-TV Foundation (USA), February–April 1962. See D(i):1962.

1968

December	'Does Faith mean Commitment . . .?'

1969

January	'And God Said . . .'
February	'Rebel and/or God'
March	'Death and Christ'
May	'Power When You Need It'
June	'In Close Touch'
October	'Quiet Intruder'

1976

January/ February	'Personal Impressions of the Nairobi Assembly'
April/May	'John Stott Visits Asia and Australia'
July/August	'Evangelicals in Conference'
November	'June to September'

1977

January/ February	'PACLA' [Pan-African Christian Leadership Assembly]
March	'John Stott in America'
April/May	'Cambridge Mission'
June	'NEAC '77: John Stott Gives a Retrospect'
July/August	'Evangelicals and Roman Catholics'
September	'John Stott in Latin America'
October/ November	'Is the Incarnation a Myth?'
December	'John Stott Visits West Africa'

1978

January/ February	'Christians and Animals'
March/April	'Gospel and Culture'
May/June	'Forward from Lausanne'
July/August	'Following Paul in Turkey'
September/ October	'Are Evangelicals Fundamentalists?'
November/ December	'The Lambeth Conference'

1980

September/ October	'Consultation on World Evangelization'

1981

January/ February	'Economic Equality among Nations: A Christian Concern?'
	'The Just Demands of Economic Inequality' reproduced from *Christianity Today*, 2 May 1980. See E(ii):Christianity Today 1977–1981, May 1980.
March/April	'The London Institute for Contemporary Christianity'

1988

July/August	'The Miracles of Jesus' Reprinted from *Essentials*, chapter 4. See A:1988.

1990

August	(This issue took the form of the All Souls Yearbook, 1990) 'New Age' Reprinted from 'Conflicting Gospels' in the *Church of England Newspaper*. See E(iii):December 1989.

1991

April	'Stott of the Antarctic'
July/August	'People who have Influenced Me'

1977–1981

CHRISTIANITY TODAY (USA) *1977–1981* 'Cornerstone' series. Some of the following appeared in the previous series, E(ii):All Souls Articles, 1972–1991.

1977

July 8	'Anglican Evangelicals Speak Out'
August 12	'Evangelicals and Roman Catholics'
September 9	'A Visit to Latin America'
October 7	'Unhooked Christians'
November 4	'Is the Incarnation a Myth?'
December 9	'English-speaking West Africa'

1978

January 13	'Church and State in England'
February 10	'Christians and Animals'
March 10	'Truth, Heresy and Discipline in the Church'
April 7	'Gospel and Culture'
May 5	'Must I really Love Myself?'
June 2	'Forward from Lausanne'
July 21	'Following Paul in Turkey'
September 8	'Are Evangelicals Fundamentalists?'
October 6	'The Lambeth Conference'
November 3	'Evangelicals in Norway'
December 1	'Christians and Muslims'

1979

January 5	'An Open Response to Arthur Johnston'
February 2	'The Christian Church in Burma'
March 23	'Transcendence: Now a Secular Quest'
April 6	'What is Human Life Anyway?'
May 4	'Reclaiming the Biblical Doctrine of Work'
June 8	'Creative by Creation: Our Need for Work'
August 17	'Challenging the Christians Down Under'
September 21	'Peacemaking is a Management Responsibility'
October 5	'Freeing a Stalwart People from Fatalism'
November 2	'Preserving the Richness of Racial Diversity'
December 7	'The Mythmakers' Myth'

1980

January 4	'The Biblical Scope of the Christian Mission'
February 8	'Calling for Peacemakers in a Nuclear Age (1)'
March 7	'Calling for Peacemakers in a Nuclear Age (2)'
April 4	'Brazil: The Spiritual Climate'
May 2	'Economic Equality Among Nations: A Christian Concern?'
May 23	'The Just Demands of Economic Inequality'
July 18	'Protestant Unity in Yugoslavia'
September 5	'Does Life Begin Before Birth?'
October 10	'Poland's Power of the Proletariat'
November 7	'Saving Souls and Serving Bread'

December 12	'Reviving Evangelism in Britain'
1981	
February 6	'Seminarians are not Tadpoles'
March 13	'Paralyzed Speakers and Hearers'
April 10	'The Problems and Promise for Evangelism in India'
May 8	'Who, then, are the Poor?'
June 12	'Jesus is Lord! has Wide Ramifications'

1977–1979

DECISION (USA) *1977–1979* 'From His Word' series.
Reprinted from *The Keswick Week 1975*. See C(ii):1975.

1977	
December	'Ephesians 1:1–14'
1978	
January	'Ephesians 1:15–18'
February	'Ephesians 1:18–23'
March	'Ephesians 2:1–10'
April	'Ephesians 2:11–22'
May	'Ephesians 3:1–13'
June	'Ephesians 3:14–21'
July	'Ephesians 4:1–6'
August	'Ephesians 4:7–16'
September	'Ephesians 4:17–25'
October	'Ephesians 4:25 – 5:4'
November	'Ephesians 5:5–21'
December	'Ephesians 5:22 – 6:24'
1979	
January	'Ephesians 5:22 – 6:24 continued'
February	'Ephesians 5:22 – 6:4'
March	'Ephesians 6:1–7'
April	'Ephesians 6:10–23'
May	'Ephesians 6:10–23 continued'

Note: Decision is published in a number of different national editions; and contents may vary slightly between editions.

1980

DECISION (USA) *1980* 'From His Word' series. Reprinted from *The Keswick Week, 1972*. See C(ii):1972.

July	'Matthew 5:1–12'
August	'Matthew 5:3–4'
September	'Matthew 5:5–6'
October	'Matthew 5:7–9'
November	'Matthew 5:9–12'
December	'The Beatitudes (concluded)'

Note: Decision is published in a number of different national editions; and contents may vary slightly between editions.

1980
SOUTHERN CROSS (AUSTRALIA) *1980*. Addresses given in St Andrew's Cathedral, Sydney, in May 1979 during the Billy Graham Crusade.

May	'The Gospel (1)'
June	'The Gospel (2)'
July	'Evangelism and the Church (1)'
August	'Evangelism and the Church (2)'
September	'Evangelism and Social Responsibility (1)'
October	'Evangelism and Social Responsibility (2)'

1988–1989
BIBLIOTHECA SACRA (USA) *1988–1989*. Series on 'Christian Ministry in the 21st Century' delivered as the W. H. Griffith Thomas Lectures at Dallas Theological Seminary, 3–6 November 1987.

1988

April/June	1. 'The World's Challenge to the Church'
July/ September	2. 'The Church's Mission in the Modern World'
October/ December	3. 'Christian Preaching in the Contemporary World'

1989

January/ March	4. 'Ideals of Pastoral Ministry'

See A:1992, *The Contemporary Christian* for Nos. 1–3; and A:1990, *The Message of Acts* for No. 4.

1992–1993
INTERVARSITY'S STUDENT LEADERSHIP (USA) *1992–1993*. Series condensed and edited from informal talks given to Latin American student leaders in 1985. See A:1992, *Los Problemas del Liderazgo Cristiano*.

1992

Fall	1. 'Revolutionizing Relationships'
Winter	2. 'Maintaining Spiritual Freshness'

1993

Spring	3. 'Persevering under Pressure'
Summer	4. 'Are you too Young to Lead?'

1992–1994

IN TOUCH 1992–1994

1992

Issue No. 2.	'Manufacturing Truth'
Issue No. 3.	'On Track'

1993

Issue No. 1.	'Timeless Truths, Clothed in Culture'
Issue No. 2.	'Let's Talk about Sex'

1994

Issue No. 1.	'Mind Matters'

(iii) Articles

1945

January/ February	*The C.S.S.M.*	'Child Conversion'

1949

January 12	*Life of Faith*	'Evangelical Hypocrisy'
Autumn	*Inter-Varsity*	'Belief on Testimony'

1950

December	*The Christian Graduate*	'The Presentation of the Gospel: Conversion and Regeneration' See E(ii): All Souls Sermons 1946–1985; June 1950.

1951

September/ October	*The Young Churchman's Bulletin*	'Hallelujah!' See E(ii):All Souls Sermons 1946–1985; July 1951.

1952

Spring	*Inter-Varsity*	'The Head of the Body'
May	*Young Life*	'I Believe in the Doctrine of the Virgin Birth (1)'
June	*Young Life*	'I Believe in the Doctrine of the Virgin Birth (2)'
Autumn	*Inter-Varsity*	'The Spirit and the Church'
December 27	*Nursing Times*	'A Christmas Sermon'

1953

January/ February	*Church and People*	'The Lord's Loaf' From a sermon at High Leigh, May 1951.
February 28	*Sunday Companion*	'Where God Rules'

| November/
December | *Missionary Messenger* | 'For All Men'
Synopsis of an address at a
BCMS Valedictory Meeting,
Kingsway Hall, September
1953. |
| December 25 | *Marylebone Mercury* | 'Where Does Christmas Begin?' |

1954

February	*In the Service of Medicine*	'The Human Body' Summary of a sermon in All Souls at a Service for Doctors, 18 October 1953. See E(ii):All Souls Sermons 1946–1985; December 1953.
March	*Bright Words*	'The Steadfast Love of God'
Spring	*London Bible College Review*	'Conversion and Regeneration' See E(iii): December 1950.
May	*Bright Words*	'The Saviour of the World'
June	*The Churchman*	'Reconciliation: an exposition of 2 Corinthians 5:18–21'
Summer	*Theological Students' Fellowship Terminal Newsletter*	'The New Testament's Use of the Old' Abstract of an address at the Theological Students' Fellowship Conference, December 1953.
September	*Bright Words*	'Jesus Christ and the Bible'
September	*The Christian Graduate*	'The Ministry of the Word' See E(iii):January 1957.

1955

January/ February	*The Church Gazette and Intelligencer*	'Once' From a sermon in All Souls, 15 October 1954.
March	*In the Service of Medicine*	'What is Man?' Summary of a sermon in All Souls at a Service for Doctors, 17 October 1954. See E(ii):All Souls Sermons 1946–1985; November 1954.
May	*The Cambridge Review*	'A Child's Humility' Resumé of a sermon before the University of Cambridge in the University Church, 1 May 1955. See E(ii):All Souls Sermons 1946–1985; July 1955.

June	*Crusade*	'Except a Man be Born Again . . .'
November	*Crusade*	'Fundamentalism' See D(ii):1956; E(iii):Spring 1956.
November/ December	*World Dominion*	'Lay Evangelism in the Home Churches'
December	*The London Churchman*	'Dynamic for What?'
December	*Crusade*	'John Stott's Christmas Quiz'
December	*Caterers' Record*	'No Room at the Inn' See E(iii):December 1970.
December 31	*Sunday Companion*	'Are You Growing Up?'

1956

January	*Crusade*	'Why do the Innocent Suffer?' See D(ii):1956.
January	*Bright Words*	'The New Covenant'
Spring	*Theological Students' Fellowship Terminal Letter*	'Are we Fundamentalists?' Compiled with the author's permission by Andrew Walls from 'two articles by John Stott': chiefly from 'Fundamentalism', *Crusade*. See E(iii):November 1955.
April 21	*Christian Herald*	'The Christian and his Enemies'
May	*Crusade*	'Evangelicals and Evangelism' See D(ii):1956, *Fundamentalism and Evangelism*.
June	*The Christian Graduate*	'The Meaning of Evangelism' See D(ii):1964.
December	*Crusade*	'John Stott's Christmas Quiz'

1957

January	*Crusade*	'The Ministry of the Word' Reprinted from *The Christian Graduate*. See E(iii):September 1954.
April	*Crusade*	'Why did Christ Die?'
April	*Tumloc*	'The late Dr Isaac Jones' Address at a Memorial Service in All Souls, 4 April 1957.
May	*Moody Monthly* (USA)	'What are Christians Like?' The substance of an address at the Moody Bible Institute during the 51st Annual Founder's Week Conference.
May	*His* (USA)	'Usurping the Glory of God'

1958

March	*Crusade*	'The Character of Christ' An extract from *Basic Christianity*. See A:1958.
March/April	*Living Waters*	'Our Meat and Drink'

1959

March	*The Christian Graduate*	'Evangelism in the Student World'
March	*Certezze* (Italy)	'Divenir Cristiani' (Becoming a Christian) See D(ii):1950.
March/April	*Practical Christianity*	'The Lord's Prayer' Reprinted from *The Lord's Prayer: a Christian Philosophy of Life*. See D(ii):1956.
Spring	*Theological Students' Fellowship Terminal Letter*	'Lambeth and Church Unity' Extracts from a sermon on the second section of the Lambeth Report, 1958.
June	*On Special Service* (Australia)	'How this Book Speaks' From an address in St Andrew's Cathedral, Sydney, for Scripture Union Week, 1958.
September	*Eternity* (USA)	'Must Christ be Lord and Savior?' A discussion between John Stott and Everett F. Harrison.
November 20	*Church Times*	'Order or Chaos in the Church's Liturgy?'
November 23	*Christianity Today* (USA)	'Christ and the Scriptures'

1960

February	*Crusade*	'The Love of God' From a sermon in All Souls. See E(ii):All Souls Sermons 1946–1985; April 1952.
February 5	*Church of England Newspaper*	'An Epiphany Meditation'
June 3	*Church of England Newspaper*	'The Activity of the Holy Spirit'
July/August	*Church and People*	'The Glory of the Cross' A sermon in St Margaret's Westminster at the Islington Clerical Conference, January 1960.

October	*His* (USA)	'Christ Trusted the Scriptures' Reprinted from *Christianity Today*. See E(iii): 23 November 1959.
November	*His* (USA)	'The Bible's Purpose' Reprinted from *Christianity Today*, See E(iii):23 November 1959.
December	*His* (USA)	'Evangelism in the Student World' Reprinted from *The Christian Graduate*. E(iii): March 1959.
December	*Crusade*	'They Met at Bethlehem' From a sermon in All Souls. See E(ii):All Souls Sermons 1946–1985; February 1958.
December 23	*Church of England Newspaper*	'Vengeance – Human and Divine'

1961

March/April	*The Church Gazette*	'An Evangelical Looks Afresh at the Sacraments' A paper given at the Evangelical Fellowship of Gloucester Diocese, July 1960.
May 26	*Church of England Newspaper*	'The Confession of an Evangelical'

1962

January	*Decision* (USA)	'The Meat of the Gospel'
January 5	*Church of England Newspaper*	'Intercommunion' See D(ii):1963.
February	*Church News*	'Intercommunion'
April 27	*Christianity Today* (USA)	'Preparing for Persecution '
June 9	*Christian Herald*	'The Secret of the Nine Graces'
July	*Crusade*	'Christian Joy' From a sermon in All Souls. See E(ii):All Souls Sermons 1946–1985; March 1962.
Summer (No. 26)	*The Oak Leaf*	'A sermon on James 4:7, 8' Preached at Oak Hill College, 24 January 1962.
October	*Inter-Varsity* (special issue)	'Jesus Christ is God'

1963

January	*Signs of the Times* (USA)	'He shall Come to Judge'

		A sermon broadcast by the Episcopal Radio-TV Foundation, Atlanta, Georgia on a national network, 18 March 1962.
January 3	*Life of Faith*	'Christian Joy'
February	*All Souls*	'The Thalidomide Acquittals'
March 22	*Church Times*	'Two articles on Prayer Book Revision: 1. Why Evangelicals are so Anxious' See D(ii):1963.
March 29	*Church Times*	'Two articles on Prayer Book Revision: 2. Amending the Prayer Book' See D(ii):1963.
April	*Crusade*	'The Power of God: An Easter Meditation' From a sermon in All Souls. See E(ii):All Souls Sermons 1946–1985; April 1962.
December	*Midwives' Chronicle*	'The Virgin Mother and her Child'

1964

| April | *Crusade* | 'Beyond the Divide'
From a sermon in All Souls. See E(ii):All Souls Sermons 1964–1985; February 1964. See C(ii):1977, *Death: Jesus made it all Different*. |

1965

| March | *Decision* (USA) | 'Teacher and Lord'
From a reply to a question at the IVCF missionary convention, Urbana 1964. See note at the foot of Section G. |
| July 30 | *The Christian* | 'Union with Christ'
From a Bible-reading at the 1965 Keswick Convention. See C(ii):1965. |

1966

| January | *Crusade* | 'Ambition'
From a sermon in All Souls. See E(ii):All Souls Sermons 1946–1985; October 1964. |

December **1970**	'Sunlight on Mist'
March	'A House not Made by Hands'

1972–1991

ALL SOULS ARTICLES 1972–1991. The following is a series of articles contributed sometimes regularly and sometimes occasionally to the magazine *All Souls.* A single earlier article of the same general nature appeared in February 1963 – see E(iii):1963. Editorials, reports, letters and domestic contributions relating primarily to the life of the church are excluded. Summaries of sermons are listed separately under E(ii):All Souls Sermons 1946–85. No distinction is made here between the magazine and the broadsheet which succeeded it in September/ October 1990.

1972

January	'Should we Scrap Confirmation?'
March	'Anglican – Roman Catholic Agreement?'
May	'Anglicans and Methodists: The Final Verdict'
July	'April in Asia'
September	'Should the Church of England be Disestablished?'
October	'John Stott Visits America'
December	'John Stott Meets Students in the States'

1973

February	'John Stott Reports on American Church Life Today'
April	'John Stott Discusses Authority and Freedom'
June	'John Stott Asks . . . Only One Way?'
August	'John Stott Travels from Tropics to Tundra'
December	'John Stott on Safari in East Africa'

1974

January	'John Stott in East Asia* and the Americas' [* a misprint for Africa]
February	'Getting our Priorities Right' Four talks on the Lord's Prayer from the BBC 'Thought for the Day', January 1974.
March	'John Stott in North and South America'
May	'John Stott Anticipates the London Lectures in Contemporary Christianity'
July	'John Stott Visits Australia, the Philippines and Taiwan'
September	'John Stott Reports on the Lausanne Congress'
November	'John Stott Comments on Lausanne and Culture'

1975

March	'John Stott Goes First East, then West'
September/ October	'Abortion in Britain'
October/ November	'Simple Lifestyle'

January	*His* (USA)	'Teacher and Lord' Reprinted from *Decision*. See E(iii):March 1965.
Vol. 3.3 (old series)	*Themelios*	'Exposition: Peace with God' Abridged from chapter 1 of *Men Made New*. See A:1966.
June	*Decision* (USA)	'A Word for Britain'
June	*Crusade*	'Rumours of Wars' From a sermon in All Souls. See E(ii):All Souls Sermons 1946–1985; January 1966.

1967

February 24	*Church of England Newspaper*	'That Word "Radical" '
March 31	*Church Times*	'National Evangelical Congress at Keele: Attempt to Face Today's Questions'
June	*His* (USA)	'A Song of Service'
October	*His* (USA)	'Preview of His Coming'
October	*Inter-Varsity*	'Resurrection: Myth or Miracle?'
November	*His* (USA)	'Under Attack' See E(iii):27 April 1962, 'Preparing for Persecution'.
December	*His* (USA)	'Three Views of the Church'
December	*Midwives' Chronicle*	'She gave Birth to Her First-born Son'

1968

January 4	*Life of Faith*	'Revival in 1968?'
April	*World Christian Digest*	'The Stumbling Block of the Cross' Reprinted from *Church Herald*. See E(ii):Church Herald 1966–1980; 29 September 1967.
April	*Crossroads* (Kuala Lumpur)	'Resurrection: Myth or Miracle?' Reprinted from *Inter-Varsity*. See E(iii):October 1967.
May 10	*Church of England Newspaper*	'Racialism versus our Common Humanity' From a sermon in All Souls, 5 May 1968.
June 7	*Church of England Newspaper*	'The Historicity of Adam'

August 16	*Church of England Newspaper*	'Two articles about the WCC Assembly at Uppsala: 1. An Evangelical at Uppsala'
August 23	*Church of England Newspaper*	'Two articles about the WCC Assembly at Uppsala: 2. Why I was Disturbed'
Autumn	*Inter-Varsity*	'Racialism versus our Common Humanity' Reprinted from the *Church of England Newspaper*. See E(iii):May 1968.
October	*His* (USA)	'Lighted Darkness'
November 1	*Church of England Newspaper*	'Evangelicals in a Changing World' Extracts from an address given to the London Diocesan Evangelical Union, October 1968.
November 8	*The Christian & Christianity Today*	'A Christian Philosophy of Life and Death' From a sermon in All Souls at a Service for Doctors, 13 October 1968. See E(ii):All Souls Sermons 1946–1985; December 1968.

1969

| April | *Crusade* | 'The Cross and the Resurrection'
From a sermon in All Souls, 29 March 1964. See E(ii):All Souls Sermons 1946–1985; June 1964. |
| November 7 | *Christianity Today* (USA) | 'When Should a Christian Weep?' |

1970

January 2	*Church of England Newspaper and Record*	'The Crisis of Authority'
January 9	*Church of England Newspaper and Record*	'What Should the Church do with False Teachers?'
February 6	*Church of England Newspaper and Record*	'The Abolition of Capital Punishment'
February 27	*Church of England Newspaper and Record*	'The Death Penalty – John Stott replies'
March 26	*Church Times*	'Historical Events and Saving Truths'
November	*Decision* (USA)	'Authentic Christianity'

December	*Molesey Review and Esher Courier*	Reprinted from *Christ the Controversialist*. See A:1970. 'No Room at the Inn' Reprinted from the *Caterers' Record*. See E(iii):December 1955.

1971

June	*His* (USA)	'Christ: Lord and Liberator'
Autumn	*The Churchman*	'The Biblical Teaching on Divorce' See D(ii):1972.
October 29	*Church of England Newspaper*	'Reverence for Human Life (1)'
November 5	*Church of England Newspaper*	'Reverence for Human Life (2)' From a sermon in All Souls at a Service for Doctors, October 1971. See D(ii):1972.

1972

March 23	*Church of England Newspaper*	'The Bible and the Crisis of Authority' An extract from the Annual Sermon of the British and Foreign Bible Society. See D(ii):1972.
March 30	*Church of England Newspaper*	'The Bible and the Crisis of Authority' A concluding extract from the Annual Sermon of the British and Foreign Bible Society – see above.
June 9	*Christianity Today* (USA)	'Reverence for Human Life' Reprinted from the *Church of England Newspaper*. See E(iii):October 1971 and November 1971.
November	*EFAC Bulletin*	'Strategy for Evangelism – Morecambe, 6th–13th May 1972'

1973

Vol. 73.2	*IFES Journal*	'Impressions of American Christianity' See E(ii):All Souls Articles 1972–1991; February 1973.
July	*EFAC Bulletin*	'A Worldwide Fellowship'

| | | Reprinted from chapter 12 of *Evangelicals Today*. See C(ii):1973. |
| September | *Decision* (USA) | 'Teacher and Lord' Reprinted from *Decision*. See E(iii):March 1965. |

1974

May	*His* (USA)	'Imprint of the Early Church'
November	*Decision* (USA)	'Five words' From an address at the International Congress on World Evangelization, Lausanne, July 1974. See also C(ii):1975, *Let the Earth hear His Voice*, 'The Biblical Basis of Evangelism'.
December	*Post American* (USA)	'Imitating the Incarnation'
December 13	*Church of England Newspaper*	'The Maturity of Love'

1975

January	*EFAC Bulletin*	'Lausanne '74' Adapted from an article in *All Souls*. See E(ii):All Souls Articles 1972–1991; September 1974.
July	*International Review of Mission*	'The Significance of Lausanne'
July 12	*Christian Herald and Signs of Our Times*	'The Believer's Maturity in Christ' Reprinted from *All Souls*. See E(ii):All Souls Sermons 1946–1985; November 1970.
August 23	*Christian Herald and Signs of Our Times*	'Peace through Pain' Reprinted from *All Souls*. See E(ii):All Souls Sermons 1946–1985; September 1971.

1976

January	*International Review of Mission*	'Response to Bishop Mortimer Arias'
March	*EFAC Bulletin*	'The World Council of Churches and Evangelism'
June	*His* (USA)	'The Greatness of His Power . . . in us who Believe' From an address at the 1975

		Keswick Convention. See C(ii):1975.
September	*Themelios*	'Paul prays for the church – Ephesians 3:14–21' See A:1979, *God's New Society*.
November	*His* (USA)	'How to View the Bible' An extract from *Guard the Gospel*. See A:1973.
November	*His* (USA)	'Teacher and Lord' Reprinted from *Decision*. See E(iii):March 1965.

1977

March	*EFAC Bulletin*	'The Christian Church in Africa'
Spring	*Kerygma* (USA)	'The Christian Church in Africa' See above: *EFAC Bulletin*, March 1977.
April 16	*Guardian*	'Face to Faith'
December 1	*Third Way*	'World Evangelization: Signs of Convergence and Divergence in Christian Understanding'

1978

| July 8 | *Christian Herald and Signs of Our Times* | 'Is it Possible for Man to Know God?' Reprinted from *All Souls*. See E(ii):All Souls Sermons 1946–1985; October/November 1977. |
| September 22 | *Church of England Newspaper* | 'Are Evangelicals Fundamentalists?' Reprinted from *All Souls*. See E(ii):All Souls Articles 1972–1991; September/October 1978. See also E(ii):Christianity Today 1977–1981; 8 September 1978. |

1979

| April | *Crusade* | 'With Christ, which is Far Better' Reprinted from *Focus on Christ*, chapter 5. See A:1979. |
| August | *Decision* (USA) | 'Like an Eagle in a Cage' Reprinted from *The Keswick Week, 1962*. See C(ii):1962. |

| August | *EFAC Bulletin* | 'Inspiration and Harmonisation'
An excerpt from the 1979 Olivier Beguin Memorial Lecture. See D(ii):1979. |
| September | *Crux* (USA) | 'The Kingdom and Community: Can the Kingdom of God Satisfy Man's Search for Love?' |

1980

January	*His* (USA)	'Romans 7: The First Step to Holiness' An extract from *Men Made New*. See A:1966.
April	*Evangelical Review of Theology*	'Reclaiming the Biblical Doctrine of Work' Reprinted from *Christianity Today*. See E(ii):Christianity Today 1977–1981; 4 May 1979.
October	*Nucleus*	'The Mystery and Mastery of Suffering' Reprinted from *All Souls*. See E(ii):All Souls Sermons 1946–1985; December 1974.
November	*Crusade*	'Nuclear Warfare in the Modern World: The Christian Option' Reprinted from an All Souls Paper. See D(i):All Souls Papers 1979–1981; 11 November 1979.

1981

February 6	*Christianity Today* (USA)	'Scripture the Light and Heat for Evangelism'
April	*Decision* (USA)	'The Bible in World Evangelization' Abridged from *Perspectives on the World Christian Movement: A Reader*. See C(ii):1981.
June 12	*Christianity Today* (USA)	'Setting the Spirit Free'
August	*EFAC Bulletin*	'Hugh Silvester'
August/ September	*Decision* (USA)	'Christian Faith' From a sermon in All Souls, 4 November 1962. See E(ii): All Souls Sermons 1946–1985; January 1963.

1982

January/ February	*Ichthus* (France)	'Pacifiques ou Pacifistes?' (Peacemakers or Pacifists?) Translated from a sermon in All Souls, November 1979, with a response by Pierre Courthial and a further reply by John Stott.
June	*His* (USA)	'Teacher and Lord' Reprinted from *Decision*. See E(iii):March 1965.
October	*Decision* (USA)	'Don't be Unreasonable' Reprinted from *The Keswick Week, 1962*. See C(ii):1962.
October	*EFAC Bulletin*	'This Way Forward: An Agenda for a new ARCIC' An extract from *Evangelical Anglicans and the Final ARCIC Report*. See D(ii):1982.
November	*His* (USA)	'Peacemaking, the Best Medicine: A Case for Nuclear Pacifism' Abridged from a sermon in All Souls, 11 November 1979. See D(i):All Souls Papers 1979– 1981; November 1979.

1983

Spring	*Tear Times*	'John Stott, Gilbert Kirby, Cliff Richard on their New Roles with Tear Fund'
Vol. 97.1	*Churchman*	'Jesus Christ, the Life of the World'
July 8	*Church of England Newspaper*	'The Death Penalty'
July 15	*Church of England Newspaper*	'Hanging – Does it Preserve Human Life?'
September 30	*Church of England Newspaper*	'Versatile Pioneer we Shall Deeply Miss: A Tribute to Myra Chave-Jones'
No. 1	*Proceedings of the Anglican Evangelical Assembly*	'A Fresh Look at Ministry in the New Testament'

1984

January/ March	*Transformation*	'Seeking Theological Agreement'

April	*Decision* (USA)	'Christian Obedience' Reprinted from *Understanding Christ*. See A:1979.
April 20	*Christianity Today* (USA)	'Am I Supposed to Love Myself or Hate Myself?'
Vol. 3.2	*East Africa Journal of Evangelical Theology* (Kenya)	'The Christian Contribution to Nation Building' Adapted from chapter 4 of *Issues Facing Christians Today*. See A:1984.

1985

Summer	*Japan Christian Quarterly*	'Communication, Context, and the Centrality of Jesus Christ' Reprinted from *Proclaiming Christ to His World*. See C(ii):1984.
April 6	*The Times*	'Reflections on the Resurrection'
July	*Evangelical Review of Theology*	'Salt and Light: the Christian Contribution to Nation Building' See E(iii):Vol. 3.2, 1984.
August 9	*Christianity Today* (USA)	'What Makes Leadership Christian?' Reprinted from chapter 9 of *Involvement*, Vol. 2. See A:1985.
August 29	*Christian Herald*	'Cross Purposes' Summary of a sermon first published in *All Souls*. See E(ii):All Souls Sermons 1946–1985; September/October 1983.
November 22	*Christianity Today* (USA)	'Homosexual Marriage' Adapted from chapter 8 of *Involvement*, Vol. 2. See A:1985.

1986

January	*International Bulletin of Missionary Research* (USA)	'The Evangelical–Roman Catholic Dialogue on Mission, 1977–1984: A Report' Edited jointly by Basil Meeking and John Stott. See B(ii):1986.
January/ March	*Collegiate Quarterly* (USA)	'God's New Society' Reprinted from *The Message of Ephesians*. See A:1984.

May	*Decision* (USA)	'The Lordship of Christ' Reprinted from *The Gospel, the Spirit, the Church*. See C(ii):1978.
July	*Focus*	'The Manner of His Coming'
Advent (Vol. 34)	*EFAC Bulletin*	'A New Beginning'

1987

January 16	*Christianity Today* (USA)	'God on the Gallows' From chapter 13 of *The Cross of Christ*. See A:1986.
Advent (No. 35)	*EFAC Bulletin*	'Kinds of Comprehensiveness' Reprinted from 'I Believe in the Church of England' in *Hope for the Church of England?* See C(ii):1986.

1988

Vol. 3.6	*Catalyst*	'A Mature Man – Dr John Laird' The address at a Thanksgiving Service, 21 April 1988.
November/ December	*World Evangelization* (USA)	'Our Challenge for Today' The keynote address of the European Leadership Conference on World Evangelization at Stuttgart, Germany, 5–9 September 1988.
1988/89 (annual)	*IFES Overview*	'The Crucial Decision' An extract from an address at the IFES European Conference on Evangelism, Wurzburg, Germany, April 1988.

1989

January	*World Evangelization* (USA)	'The Lausanne Covenant: an Exposition and Commentary' See D(ii):1975; E(iv):1989.
March/April	*World Evangelization* (USA)	'Evangelism through the Local Church: an Exposition of 1 Thessalonians 1:5–10' Rewritten as part of chapter 1 in *The Message of Thessalonians*. See A:1991.
Pentecost (Vol. 38)	*EFAC Bulletin*	'The President says Goodbye to Vinay Samuel' 'Retreats for Anglican Leaders'

May	*World Christian* (USA)	'John Stott on Hell' Reprinted from John Stott's Response to chapter 6 of *Evangelical Essentials*. See A:1989.
June	*TableTalk* (USA)	'The Problem of Forgiveness' Reprinted from *The Cross of Christ*. See A:1986.
July/October	*Care News*	'Don't Give Up!' From chapter 17 of *Issues Facing Christians Today*. See A:1984.
Summer	*Tear Times*	'Undaunted in Uganda'
September/ October	*All Souls*	'Introduction to Ecclesiastes' 'Atheism – its Futility' Two short summaries of sermons in All Souls, April 1989.
December 8	*Church of England Newspaper*	'Conflicting Gospels'

1990

January/ February/ March	*InCourage* (Canada)	'Farewell to Vinay Samuel'
June/July	*East Asia Millions*	'What I Learned from Hudson Taylor'
Autumn	*Tear Times*	'Why Care for the Planet?' Abridged from chapter 6 of *Issues Facing Christians Today*. See A:1984.
Fall	*Presbyterion* (USA)	'A Response to Professor Robert L. Reymond'

1990/91

| December 1990/ January 1991 | *Third Way* | 'The Glory and the Shame' The address at the National Prayer Breakfast, 22 November 1989. See D(ii):1989 *What is Man?* |

1991

| February 2 | *Christian Herald* | 'Know the Times' Abridged from an interview in *Idea*, November/December 1990. See E(iv):November/ December 1990. |
| September | *Crux* (USA) | 'Secular Challenges to the Contemporary Church' |

Based on a lecture at the Summer School of Regent College, Vancouver, June 1991, chapter 14 of *The Contemporary Christian*. See A:1992.

1992

August 17	*Christianity Today* (USA)	'The Unforbidden Fruit' See A:1992, *The Contemporary Christian*, chapter 9.

1993

January	*Evangelical Review of Theology*	'The Authentic Jesus' Abridged from *The Authentic Jesus*. See A:1985.
Summer	*Tear Times*	'Why Christian Mission is Holistic' Abridged from chapter 20 of *The Contemporary Christian*. See A:1992.
June	*Insight* (USA)	'The Contemporary Christian' An address to the Convocation of Wycliffe College, Toronto, 10 May 1993, on receiving an honorary doctorate.
July/August	*Decision* (USA)	'Taking in, Giving out' Reprinted from *Baptism and Fullness*. See A:1975.
September	*Crux* (USA)	'A Dialogue on Christian Sexual Ethics' A transcript of the debate between John Stott and Bishop J. S. Spong in Christ Church Cathedral, Vancouver, 7 July 1993.

1994

January	*Evangelical Review of Theology*	'The Logic of Hell: a Brief Rejoinder' John Stott's short response to an article 'The Logic of Hell: a Response to Annihilationism' by Simon Chan, in the same issue.
February	*Crossword*	Included as supplement to this issue, a shortened version of *The Church and the Moral Order*

		containing a digest of the contribution by John Stott, 'Homosexual Partnerships'. See D(iii):1994.
Summer (No. 8)	*Christian Impact Newsletter*	'Ernest Lucas: an Appreciation'
December 1994/ January 1995	*World Evangelization*	'The Lausanne Covenant: 20 years'

(iv) Interviews

1974

May	*Crusade*	'People in Close-Up: John Capon talks to John Stott (1)'
June	*Crusade*	'People in Close-Up: John Capon talks to John Stott (2)'

1975

August/ September	*The Evangelical Magazine of Wales*	'Interview' with Dr Brian Harris, editor.
October	*His* (USA)	'A *His* interview with John R. W. Stott'

1976

February 20	*Church Herald* (USA)	'What's the State of the Gospel?' Interview with John Stapert, editor. See E(ii):Church Herald 1966–1980; 20 February 1976.

1977

June	*Crusade*	'People in Close-Up: the Cambridge Nine' Interview with Mary Endersbee.

1982

February	*Third Way*	'Struggling with Contemporary Issues' Alex Mitchell talks to John Stott.

1983

October/ November	*The Wittenberg Door* (USA)	'*Door* Interview with John Stott'

1985

| October | *Mission Journal* (USA) | 'The Church in the Modern World: An Interview with J. R. W. Stott by David A. Sampson' |

1986

| March | *Southern Cross* (Australia) | 'Stott on Students' Interview with Archbishop Donald Robinson and with *Southern Cross.* |

1987

| August/ September | *Impact* (Singapore) | 'A Call to Balanced, Biblical Christianity' Interview with editor. |
| November/ December | *World Evangelization* (USA) | 'With John Stott' Interview by Thomas Wang. |

1988

| August | *Africa Enterprise Update* (Pietermaritzburgh) | 'Michael Cassidy Interviews John Stott' Reprinted in *The Lordship of Christ in South Africa*. See A:1990. |

1989

January	*World Evangelization* (USA)	'The Lausanne Covenant Today – John Stott answers questions from Thomas Wang'
March/April	*Preaching* (USA)	'Creating the Bridge: an Interview with John R. W. Stott' Interview with R. Albert Mohler Jr.
October	*World Christian* (USA)	'Learning to Fly Kites: *World Christian* Interviews John Stott'

1990

| January/ February/ March | *InCourage* (Canada) | 'An Interview with John Stott' Interview with Stephen Andrews. |
| November/ December | *Idea* | 'John Stott: State of Play' Interview with Ian Coffey. |

1991

| November 29 | *Santalen* (Norway) | 'Vi må forkynne en dagsaktuell Kristus' |

(We Must Proclaim a Christ
Relevant for Today)
Interview with Jan Eikeland.

1992

Summer   *Church Renewal Forum*   'Interview with John Stott'
                (Hong Kong)   By Lawrence Chan (published
                                                 in Chinese).

1993

February 8   *Christianity Today* (USA)   'John Stott Speaks Out'
                                                 Interview with Michael G.
                                                 Maudlin.
No. 4; 2:1993   *Aletheia* (Spain)   'Entrevista al Dr John Stott'
                                                 (Interview with Dr John Stott)
                                                 Interview by Dr Pablo
                                                 Martínez.

1994

May/June   *Izvori* (Croatia)   'Ispovjednik Englieske Kraljice'
                                                 (The Confessor [i.e. Chaplain]
                                                 of the English Queen)
                                                 Interview with Dražen Glavaš.
July/August   *Crestinul Azi* (Romania)   'De vorbă cu . . . John Stott:
                                                 Doar când Isus este Domnul
                                                 nostru, noi suntem completi'
                                                 (Talking with . . . John Stott:
                                                 Only when Jesus is our Lord
                                                 are we Complete)
                                                 Interview with Pastor Ionel
                                                 Tujac.

(v) Reviews

1965

September   *Church of England*   *All in Each Place: Ten Anglican*
                Newspaper   *Essays with some Free Church*
                                                 Comments
                                                 Editor: J. I. Packer.
                                                 Abingdon: Marcham Manor
                                                 Press, 1963.

1971

March   *Christian Graduate*   *Evangelism in the Early Church*
                                                 By Michael Green.
                                                 London: Hodder & Stoughton,
                                                 1970.

June	*EFAC Bulletin*	*Evangelism in the Early Church* By Michael Green. London: Hodder & Stoughton, 1970. Reprinted from *Christian Graduate*, March 1970. See above.
December 3	*Church of England Newspaper*	*Preaching and Preachers* By D. Martyn Lloyd-Jones. London: Hodder & Stoughton, 1971.
December 30	*Church of England Newspaper*	*Bible Characters and Doctrines, Vols. 1 & 2* London: Scripture Union, 1971.

1972

September 1	*Church of England Newspaper*	*Highlights of the Book of Revelation* By G. R. Beasley-Murray. Nashville: Broadman Press, 1971.

1973

October	*All Souls*	*Evangelicals Today* Editor: John King. London: Lutterworth, 1973.
October	*All Souls*	*A Lawyer among the Theologians* By Norman Anderson. London: Hodder & Stoughton, 1973.
November	*EFAC Bulletin*	*Evangelicals Today* Editor: John King. London: Lutterworth, 1973. Reprinted from *All Souls*, October 1973. See above.
November	*EFAC Bulletin*	*A Lawyer among the Theologians* By Norman Anderson. London: Hodder & Stoughton, 1973. Reprinted from *All Souls*, October 1973. See above.

1976

December	*All Souls*	*Issues of Life and Death* By Norman Anderson. London: Hodder & Stoughton, 1976.

1978

| September | *Christianity Today* (USA) | *Fundamentalism*
By James Barr.
London: SCM Press, 1977. See E(ii):Christianity Today 1977–1981. |
| September/
October | *All Souls* | *Fundamentalism*
By James Barr.
London: SCM Press, 1977. See immediately above. |

1979

| January | *Occasional Bulletin of Missionary Research* (Canada) | *Christian Mission and Social Justice*
By Samuel Escobar and John Driver.
Ontario: Herald Press, 1978. |

1981

| Spring | *Trinity Journal* (USA) | *Dynamics of Spiritual Life: an Evangelical Theology of Renewal*
By Richard F. Lovelace.
Downers Grove: IVP, 1979. |

1984

| July/
September | *Transformation* | *Darkening Valley: A Biblical Perspective on Nuclear War*
By Dale Aukerman.
New York: Seabury Press, 1981. |
| Autumn | *Evangel* | *Mere Morality*
By Lewis B. Smedes.
Exeter: Paternoster, 1983. |

1985

| October | *Third Way* | *What's Right with Feminism?*
By Elaine Storkey.
London: SPCK, 1985. |
| Vol. 99.4 | *Churchman* | *Christ's Lordship and Religious Pluralism*
Editors: Gerald H. Anderson and Thomas F. Stransky.
Maryknoll: Orbis, 1981 (revised 1983). |

1986

Advent   *EFAC Bulletin*   *The Gospel Conspiracy in the*
(Vol. 34)   *Episcopal Church*
                                         By Michael Marshall.
                                         Harrisburg: Morehouse-Barlow,
                                         1986.

1990

Pentecost   *EFAC Bulletin*   *Michael Ramsey: a Life*
(No. 40)   By Owen Chadwick.
                                         Oxford: Clarendon Press, 1990.

F: Prayers

The number in brackets that *follows* the title of each prayer shows where
the same prayer is repeated in different collections. Prayers are often
reprinted with minor variations and these are not taken into account.

The number *before* each prayer, in collections of prayers, is the number
given by the editor. Where there is no number in a collection (*e.g. New
Every Morning*) the page number is given, followed by a number
indicating whether the prayer is the first, second, third, *etc.* of the prayers
on that page. Thus 'The peace of the world' is prefixed with 43.4,
indicating that it is the fourth prayer on page 43.

1950

Becoming a   See D(ii):1950.
Christian   A prayer of faith (1)

1958

Basic   See A:1958.
Christianity   A prayer of faith (1)
Your   See A:1958.
Confirmation   A prayer of faith (1)

1967

Parish Prayers London: Hodder & Stoughton, 1967.
                  Editor: Frank Colquhoun.
                     51. Before a Carol Service (2)
                    305. Easter Day: evening (3)
                    671. Mothers (4)
                    772. Children (5)
                    919. Holy Communion (6)
                   1226. Marriage (7)
                   1244. Those on holiday (8)
                   1266. The sick in body (9)
                   1324. The revival of the Church (10)

1388. Church and nation (11)
1425. The parish (12)
1439. Worship and witness (13)
1559. Love (14)
1639. Daily work (15)
1787. Music and worship (16)
1793. A sale of work (17)

1973

New Every Morning   London: British Broadcasting Corporation, new edition 1973.
Editor: Frank Colquhoun.
  43.4 The peace of the world (18)
  47.1 Liberty (19)
  86.4 Those in trouble (20)
  113.1 Our use of freedom (21)

1975

Contemporary Parish Prayers   London: Hodder & Stoughton, 1975.
Editor: Frank Colquhoun.
  290. The peace of the world (18)
  406. Those in trouble (20)

1982

New Parish Prayers   London: Hodder & Stoughton, 1982.
Editor: Frank Colquhoun.
  202. The nation's spiritual needs (22)

1986

The Hodder Book of Christian Prayers   London: Hodder & Stoughton, 1986.
Editor: Tony Castle.
  274. Love (14)
  608. Church and nation (11)
  713. Easter Day: evening (3)
  763. Children (5)
  972. Those in trouble (20)

1987

Prayers in Church   Oxford: Oxford University Press, 1987.
Editor: John Conacher.
  476. The peace of the world (18)

1993

A Treasury of Prayer   London: Hodder & Stoughton, 1993.
Editor: Tony Castle.
  134. Easter Day: evening (3)
  450. Love (14)

588. The nation's spiritual needs (22)
698. Those in trouble (20)

G: Verse and Hymns

1945

Christ Church   'A Young Man's Testimony in Verse' unsigned, but
Chronicle   written by John Stott in 1938. Six stanzas.
(of Christ
Church,
Southport)
August 1945

1946

All Souls   'A Schoolboy's Testimony in Verse' as above; but three
October 1946   stanzas only.

1953

All Souls   'Thou Callest Clear'
May 1953   The conclusion of a sermon on 'The Christian Life'. The
same five stanzas conclude the chapter 'Counting the
Cost' in *Basic Christianity*. See A:1958. In the 1971 revision
of the book, the verses are slightly recast from 'Thee' into
'You' form.

1958

Basic   'Thou Callest Clear'
Christianity   See above, and A:1958.

1963

The Christian   Hymn text: 'Anna was a Prophetess'.
20 December   To music by John Fear.
1963

1965

University   Brighton: H. Freeman & Co.
Carol Book   Editor: Erik Routley
No. 49   Hymn text: Song of Simeon: 'Dear Child, I Take Thee in
my Arms'.
To music by John Fear. See G:1985 below.

1966

The Canticles   See A:1966.
and Selected   'A Christmas Anthem'
Psalms

1985

Music in   'Dear Child, I Take Thee in my Arms'.
Worship   Published as an insert in this issue, and as sheet music
June/July   available from the Music in Worship Trust, to a tune by
1985   Robin Sheldon. See G:1965 above.

The free verse, 'Teacher and Lord' (see Index of Titles for various
reprintings) was put into that form by the editors *of Decision*, March 1965,
from John Stott's extempore reply to a question at the IVCF missionary
convention, Urbana, 1964.

Periodicals with Special Associations

Aletheia (Spain)	Alianza Evangélica Española.
All Souls	All Souls Church, Langham Place, London.
Bibliotheca Sacra	Dallas Theological Seminary, USA.
Bright Words	The Faith Mission.
Care	Care Trust and Care Campaigns.
Catalyst	Scripture Union International Information Exchange.
Certezze (Italy)	Gruppi Biblici Universitari.
Christian Graduate	Graduates' Fellowship of the Inter-Varsity Fellowship.
Christian Impact Newsletter	Christian Impact and the London Institute for Contemporary Christianity.
Church & People	Church Pastoral-Aid Society.
Church Gazette and Intelligencer	The Church Society.
Church Herald	Reformed Church in America.
Collegiate Quarterly	North American Church Ministries.
Creştinul Azi (Romania)	Baptist Churches of Romania.
Crossroads (Kuala Lumpur)	Fellowship of Evangelical Students of West Malaysia.
Crossword	Lutheran Bible Institute in California.
Crux	Regent College, Vancouver, Canada.
CSSM	Children's Special Service Mission.
Decision	Billy Graham Evangelistic Association, USA.
East Asia Millions	Overseas Missionary Fellowship.
EFAC Bulletin	Evangelical Fellowship in the Anglican Communion.
Evangelical Review of Theology	World Evangelical Fellowship Theological Commission.
Focus	Seventh Day Adventists.
His	InterVarsity Christian Fellowship, USA.
Idea	Evangelical Alliance.
IFES Journal	International Fellowship of Evangelical Students.

Insight	Wycliffe College, Toronto.
In the Service of Medicine	Christian Medical Fellowship.
International Bulletin of Missionary Research	Overseas Ministry Study Center, New Jersey, USA.
Inter-Varsity	Inter-Varsity Fellowship.
InterVarsity's Student Leadership	InterVarsity Christian Fellowship, USA.
In Touch	International Fellowship of Evangelical Students.
Kerygma	Originally published by the Fellowship of Witness, the American branch of the Evangelical Fellowship in the Anglican Communion; but later (as *Mission and Ministry*) by Trinity Episcopal School for Ministry, Ambridge, PA.
Living Waters	Living Waters Missionary Union.
London Bible College Review	London Bible College.
London Churchman, The	Diocese of London.
Meteor, The	Rugby School.
Missiology	American Society of Missiology.
Missionary Messenger	Bible Churchmen's Missionary Society.
Moody Monthly	Moody Bible Institute, USA.
Music in Worship	Music in Worship Trust.
Nucleus	Christian Medical Fellowship.
Occasional Bulletin of Missionary Research	Overseas Ministries Study Center, New Jersey, USA.
Oak Leaf, The	Oak Hill Theological College.
On Special Service	Scripture Union, Australia.
PostAmerican	The People's Christian Coalition, USA.
Practical Christianity	Officers' Christian Union.
Presbyterion	Covenant Theological Seminary, Missouri, USA.
Proceedings of the Anglican Evangelical Assembly	Church of England Evangelical Council.
Santalen (Norway)	The Norwegian Santal Mission.
Signs of the Times	Seventh Day Adventist Church, USA.
Southern Cross	The Diocese of Sydney, Australia.
TableTalk	Ligonier Ministries, Inc., USA.

Tear Times	The Evangelical Alliance Relief Fund.
Themelios	International Fellowship of Evangelical Students.
Theological Students' *Fellowship Terminal Newsletter*	Theological Students' Fellowship of the Inter-Varsity Fellowship.
Transformation	Oxford Centre for Mission Studies.
Trinity Journal	Trinity Evangelical Divinity School, Deerfield, Illinois, USA.
Tumloc	Colonial Mutual Life Assurance Society, Ltd.
World Evangelization	Lausanne Committee for World Evangelization.
Young Churchman's Bulletin	Young Churchmen's Movement of the Church Society.
Young Life	National Young Life Campaign.

Alphabetical Index of Titles

Pacifiques ou Pacifistes? E(iii):January/February 1982.

PACLA (Pan-African Christian Leadership Assembly) E(ii):All Souls Articles 1972–1991; January/February 1977.

Paralyzed Speakers and Hearers E(ii):Christianity Today 1977–1981; 13 March 1981.

Parish, The F:1967.

Parish Prayers F:1967.

Parochial Evangelism by the Laity D(ii):1952.

Paroxysm of Paul, The E(ii):All Souls Sermons 1946–1985; November 1962.

Pasadena Consultation, The: Homogeneous Unit Principle D(iii):1978.

Patient Continuance in Well-Doing E(ii):All Souls Sermons 1946–1985; July 1965.

Paul Prays for the Church E(iii):September 1976.

Paul's Apostolic Sufferings E(ii):Life of Faith 1965; 9 December 1965.

Paul's Concluding Admonitions E(ii):Life of Faith 1965; 23 December 1965.

Paul's Concluding Exhortations E(ii):Life of Faith 1965; 30 December 1965.

Paul's Defence of his Apostleship E(ii):Life of Faith 1965; 25 November 1965.

Paul's Evangelistic Zeal E(ii):Life of Faith 1965; 2 December 1965.

Paul's Final Charge E(ii):All Souls Sermons 1946–1985; January 1968.

Paul's View of the Body E(ii):In the Service of Medicine 1965; April 1965.

Payton Lectures A:1961.

Peacemakers E(ii):All Souls Sermons 1946–1985; January 1969.

Peacemakers: Christian Voices from the New Abolitionist Movement C(ii):1983.

Peacemakers or Pacifists? (French) E(iii):January/February 1982.

Peacemaking is a Management Responsibility E(ii):Christianity Today 1977–1981; 21 September 1979.

Peacemaking, the Best Medicine: A Case for Nuclear Pacifism E(iii):November 1982.

Peace of the World, The F:1973.

Peace of the World, The F:1975.

Peace of the World, The F:1987.

Peace through Pain E(ii):All Souls Sermons 1946–1985; September 1971.

Speaking the Truth in Love (Norwegian)	C(ii):1990.
Spirit and the Church, The	E(iii):Autumn 1952.
Spirit in the Believer, The	C(ii):1972.
Spirit's Message to the Church, The	E(ii):All Souls Sermons 1946–1985; November 1969.
Spirits of Just Men made Perfect	E(ii):All Souls Sermons 1946–1985; February 1964.
Spirit, the Church and the World, The	A:1990.
Spiritual Depression	E(ii):All Souls Sermons 1946–1985; August 1954.
Spiritual Gifts	E(ii):Life of Faith 1963–1964; 28 November 1963.
Spiritual Weapons for Spiritual Warfare	E(ii):All Souls Sermons 1946–1985; May/ June 1975.
Standing in Grace	E(ii):All Souls Sermons 1946–1985; July/ August 1979.
Steadfast Love of God, The	E(ii):All Souls Sermons 1946–1985; October 1953.
Steadfast Love of God, The	E(iii):March 1954.
Stepping Stones: Joint Essays on Anglican Catholic and Evangelical Unity	B(ii):1987.
Stepping Stones: Joint Essays on Anglican Catholic and Evangelical Unity	C(i):1987.
Stepping Stones: Joint Essays on Anglican Catholic and Evangelical Unity	C(ii):1987.
Stirring Invitation, A	E(ii):All Souls Sermons 1946–1985; August 1946.
Story of the New Testament, The	A:1978.
Story of the Old Testament, The	A:1978.
Stott, John	*see under* John Stott.
Stott of the Antarctic	E(ii):All Souls Articles 1972–1991; April 1991.
Stott on Students	E(iv):March 1986.
Strategy for Evangelism – Morecambe, 6th–13th May, 1972	E(iii):November 1972.
Strategy of Satan, The	E(ii):All Souls Sermons 1946–1985; August 1948.
Strategy of Satan, The	E(ii):All Souls Sermons 1946–1985; September 1962.